SO-FAJ-890

Complimentary

fine tuning

Signed—
Dean
Finney
$18.00

fine tuning

ONE MAN'S LIFE

Dean Finney (signature)

Dean Finney

Dunmore Publishing
Lexington, Virginia

Copyright © 2001 by E. Dean Finney

ALL RIGHTS RESERVED

This book may not be reproduced in whole or part without written permission from the publisher, except by a reveiwer who may quote brief passages in a review; nor may any part of this book be reproduced, stored in a retrieval system, or transmitted in any form or by any means electronic, mechanical, photocopying, recording, or other, without written permission from the publisher.

For information about this book, write to:
Dunmore Publishing
P.O. Box 57
Lexington, VA 24450-3755

ISBN 0-9710758-0-8

Manufactured in the United States of America
by Daamen Printing, West Rutland, Vermont

FIRST EDITION

In Memory

Sarah Margaret Boswell Finney
September 11, 1892 – June 26, 1991

Dedicated to my daughters
Melissa Lee and Cynthia Deanne
with great love, respect, and pride

Contents

Introduction

I sped north on I-91 on a bitingly cold day in early January 1978. The Green Mountains, their towering evergreens drooping with fresh snow, provided the only refreshing distraction.

Leaving home had been difficult; the short, restrained conversation with my wife; the lump in my throat. I took one last glance around our beautiful home, gave a reassuring pat to Corky, our cocker spaniel, curled on the love seat. I turned and left, not knowing how it would all end.

My foot hit the gas pedal heavily as if to speed the process. I was already consumed and burdened by my tumultuous decision, and I was highly conscious of the consequences that would surely haunt me. I felt a mixture of relief and regret, of confidence and concern. I sorely needed quiet time to sort things out.

I was determined to turn my life around but figured family and friends would see this only as a midlife crisis. My adventurous search for a new life and the real me had begun. Adrift in a sea of shock, I worried most about my two beloved daughters. The road ahead looked rough. I could only hope — and pray.

My immediate destination was a five-room cottage on the shores of Lake Memphremagog, a Kenneth Roberts favorite straddling the Vermont-Canadian border. The cottage — plain, but comfortable — was a far cry from the wonderful home, built years ago, that I had just left. It was privately located on a dead-end road with an attractive front lawn and beachfront.

I pulled back the drapes on the sliding glass doors and wandered out to the deck. The view was spectacular; mountains encompassed the lake as far as I could see. Slow-moving, billowy clouds painted by a brilliant sunset added an artist's touch to the scene. Fishing shanties were clustered on the ice-covered lake near a small island. A single car was slowly moving over the ice toward the shore.

What had I done? Why was I here? Who am I? Where am I going? How do I get there? The questions went on without answers. I was tired, depressed, and yet strangely serene and determined.

I knew that tongues would wag and gossip would spread, but I couldn't control that. Employees and friends might think the news incredulous; many would guess the outcome. Some would choose sides. I needed a respite from the fast-paced confrontational life I had been living, and relief from the procrastination that had been dragging me down. I certainly couldn't have envisioned the scope of the emotional potholes in the road ahead of me. My life was undergoing a traumatic twist — for better or worse?

Sure, I felt guilt and sorrow at leaving my wife of thirty-one years. Understandably she was shocked, angry, and jealous. I was sorry, but not deterred by that.

I went to bed early, tossing and turning. My final words to our counselor and friend returned to me. "The decision is made," I said. "It has been a long time coming. Your efforts on behalf of both of us in this difficult time are appreciated, but separation is the only course at this point."

He emphasized that his counsel had aimed at assessing the marriage, hoping to help us preserve it. Failing that, it was his intent and obligation to prepare and help both parties for the alternate course. I took his extended hand.

"What are your plans?" he added.

"Get away — not too far — I can't. Make the needed decisions and fulfill my responsibilities. I am pretty sure a courtroom will dictate some."

"You love it here. What about your radio stations?"

"I'm only sure of one thing at this point. I have changed. Selfishly, I want to live differently — without tension, be happy and productive in whatever challenge I decide on. Strange, but I think I will be more unselfish. I just can't go on living this charade any longer."

I worried about my daughters. Home for the holidays, they became aware of the pending plight. The older one burst into tears, ran out the back door, and lunged onto a snowbank, crying her heart out. Tears and talk followed inside. I would do nothing to hurt my loved ones, but I did — immeasurably. It wasn't the time for explanations. It was time to leave.

My beloved mother would be heartbroken and sadly find my conduct in conflict with her own values. My older brother and his wife in Greenwich just might understand. My younger brother and his wife in Philadelphia wouldn't have a clue, since we met only at family weddings, funerals, or a rare special occasion. My uncle and his wife in Vermont would swing with it and understand.

Only one person knew where I was at this critical moment. Two important mitigating factors were now in my life to ease the struggle — love and faith.

"We have our entrances and our exits," as Shakespeare wrote. Masks often hide the real person, whether a star or a minor player. This is the story of an ordinary bit player taking off his mask, revealing himself, and saying what is really important to him before the curtain is finally drawn.

one

The Early Years

There be things the good of which and the use of
which are beyond all calculations of worldly goods
and earthly uses, things such as love and honor,
which cannot be bought for a price, and which do not
die at death.

JULIANA H. EWING

Our family lived in a white shingled, four-bedroom home in a middle-class neighborhood of Greenwich, Connecticut. There was an open front porch, a full-length stone chimney on one side, and a long sloping front lawn. The straight bluestone driveway intersected a main residential street a few blocks from the main business district. Shade trees dotted the property.

A two-car garage housed Dad's Nash, and Mother's two-door, tan rumble seat Essex. Mother had a green thumb — there were colorful flower beds and a productive vegetable garden. She had obviously been influenced by her mother who had her own extensive showplace garden. My father's parents lived a block away in a large older home.

Buckfield also played an important role in those early years. Some ninety wooded acres in an area known as Round Hill were located not far from the home where Dad was born. Buckfield was an attractive woodland with stone fences, an abundant spring, wildflowers, and some stray apple trees in a grassy grove. I remember hiking a short distance to a large showy farm nearby to see the caged foxes, soon to be quarry for fancy hunters on horses and their barking hounds.

Buckfield was a welcome family retreat, instilling real love for the outdoors in me and my older brother, Warner. Dad and some professional friends built a sizable cabin with a stone fireplace, pantry, and porch. It was a mecca for family outings, and our time there strengthened family bonds.

We often celebrated the Fourth of July at our grandparents' home nearby where we enjoyed Nana's special chicken pie with gravy. Then Grandpa and Dad lit up the sky with a mix of Roman candles and skyrockets. I always remember tall and stately Grandpa dressed for office or church with shiny black shoes, gray spats, vest, gold watch and chain. He looked the gentleman he was. I would know him much longer and better than I knew my own father.

Family vacation trips in the summer often took us to Lake Minnewaska in the Shawangunk Mountains eighty miles north of New York City. The pristine lake was spectacularly nestled between craggy cliffs and lofty evergreens. The Wildmere and the Cliff House, two rambling wooden Victorian hotels, looked down on the inviting water.

The hotels were owned and operated by the Smileys, a remarkable Quaker family. The resort encompassed thousands of acres. I loved when we explored this vast domain on family hikes and carriage rides. We often took a pine-strewn trail around the lake, past gray log summerhouses with a bench that offered awesome views. I was always in a hurry to reach our "double decker" on an overhang overlooking the blue water. I remember the cautionary warnings from Mother not to lean on the railing: "It's a long way down." I learned to swim in that lake of endless depth.

My love for tennis started on the clay tennis courts at the Wildmere. Dad and Mother loved the game, and both were fine players. They often played in tournaments, and they were good instructors too. The family putting and croquet tournaments on the green at the nearby Cliff House were always fun, but they never teed any future interest in golf for me.

The rustic Wayside gift shop between the old hotels offered snacks as well. Their "purple cows" (ginger ale and grape juice) and candy bars drew my attention. Now and then I acted in a play at the hotel when they needed a kid to play a part.

Our home in Greenwich was graced with a lively succession of Boston bullterriers: Mitzi, Ginger, Buster, and Breeze. One friendly, shorthaired, mixed breed, Brownie, followed. They romped around our home and yard and loved the days at Buckfield.

One afternoon Buster was lost to a speeding car in front of the house. I cried my heart out. When Breeze died I held a private service for him, burying him in the woods at Buckfield. His grave was marked with a piece of Vermont marble as a headstone with my roughly etched inscription. I put some pretty wildflowers near it.

Once I jumped off a neighbor's shed roof, stumbled, and startled a passing dog. He pounced on me, delivering scratches, a bite, and blood until some friends warded him off. It was off to Dr. Close for a shot and treatment. I didn't blame the dog. He was scared too. I got off with a lecture that reminded me of similar scoldings: when I climbed the big maple tree in the backyard, when I knocked over a grandfather clock in the hall, when I arranged the end to a violin to get out of the squeaky, sissy lessons in school.

My dad, W. Stanley Finney, was a lawyer. At seventeen

he entered New York University Law School, and covered
the three-year course in less time. He was on the debating
team. Before that he attended a small country schoolhouse,
and then Greenwich Academy, a private school. Dad took
postgraduate courses and worked in his father's growing
private insurance business until he was old enough to practice law. In 1914 he married Sarah Margaret Boswell, the
daughter of a drugstore owner.

He was admitted to the Connecticut Bar in 1915, became Deputy Judge of the Greenwich Borough Court in
1925, and was the first judge of the Greenwich Small Claims
Court. He served in the Lower House of the Connecticut
General Assembly in 1929 and 1930, serving on judicial
and education committees. He was considered a rising star
among Republicans.

Warner was born in 1919, followed by me in 1923. Then
Mother became pregnant, and a third son, Graham, was born
in September 1930. But things soon took a dark and unexpected turn for our family. Dad was diagnosed with kidney
cancer and entered the Columbia-Presbyterian Medical Center in New York City to wage a difficult half-year battle against
the disease.

Mother commuted and lived in an adjacent room much
of the time. My grandfather helped us add a room to our
third-floor attic and Mary, a genial Irish woman, moved in
to help Mother with everything — including a new baby
boy.

We missed Dad. I didn't understand how bad it was. I
remember the trips to the city to see him. Nick usually drove
us in my grandparents' shiny black LaSalle. He did their
lawn and garden work and was an okay guy. We often visited with Dad on a roof garden where they wheeled him
from his room at the hospital. Sometimes Mom was already
there. I used to get scared looking down on the city streets

and kept away from the edge. Dad underwent and survived critical major surgery in October.

He finally returned home to recuperate and hopefully to get on with life. He looked thin and tired, but it was so good to have him back. We had missed him terribly.

The last time I saw my father alive, I was seven, and he was only thirty-eight. He was settled in his favorite brown armchair next to the radio, reading a newspaper. I leaned down, gently put his slippers on, and positioned his feet on the small footstool.

It was miserable and cold outside, and we had a fire in the fireplace. It crackled and spit sparks. The room was warm. Mom was upstairs with my new baby brother, and my older brother was probably doing his homework.

"Did you boys get the snow off the front steps?"

"We did, but it's still coming down. We'll get it in the morning before school," I replied.

"Good, don't want anyone slipping on those cement steps. I'm counting on you boys to continue to help all you can until I get back in shape. Your mother has a handful now with your baby brother. Okay? Off to bed — school tomorrow."

"Maybe not, if it keeps snowing like I hope it will."

"Just make sure the steps are clear."

"Good night, Dad. See you in the morning."

I went over and gave him a big hug. Our dog licked his brown leather slippers and bounded upstairs with me. I wondered how long it would be before we would have good times with my father again.

He was a good father — loved Mom and all of us. And we loved him very much. He never had a bad tongue; he worked hard but made time for the family. Dad was medium in height with an athletic build. His receding dark hair was cut short. He wore dark wire-rimmed glasses. He was lightning fast on a tennis court in white cotton ducks.

I can't recall any spankings, but I probably earned a few. We were always together on weekends doing chores around the house, going to the beach, or taking a trip to Buckfield for a cookout and a hike. He used to take us to catch snappers in Long Island Sound when there was a good run. The family vacation trips were always fun. I thought about these good times as I tried to fall asleep that night.

It happened suddenly. Dad suffered a relapse and returned to the hospital. He died on January 25, 1931. I didn't understand. Why, God? Why? Mom tried to comfort me. I went to my room, and I cried. How will we all live now? What are we going to do without him?

Mother just kept going in her regular loving and caring way. Maybe she knew all that time that Dad was not going to make it. I just don't know. She had reason to be emotionally and physically drained. She had lost her beloved husband and had a newborn baby and two young sons. She now had to carry the total burden of family responsibility.

Lots of flowers arrived and all kinds of people came to the house. I sat on the stairs and watched. I didn't go to the funeral, "full to overflowing" at the Second Congregational Church. Maybe they figured I would cry too much. I stayed home with Marbles, Dad's secretary, nicknamed for her regular Thursday night visits when Mom was at the hospital. We usually played marbles on the living-room floor. She was like family and a real straight shooter.

The *Greenwich Press* quoted the pastor who spoke of the "unspeakable loss that has come to this community. He was one of the finest young men, clean, honest, intelligent, and efficient. Our life is not measured by lengths of years, but what we think, and feel, and do. Many lives are lived twice as long, but have not achieved as much in service, nor in admiration and affection of the community."

He was gone for good. I couldn't believe it. Mother received a letter from Dad's primary nurse at the New York hospital. She wrote: "I have hesitated to write fearing my letter would be too painful a reminder. I have thought so often of you and the boys. I do not wish to flatter you, but you stand apart in my mind from the rest of womankind, for reasons I will not enumerate. . . . The babe is certainly adorable. He must certainly be a great consolation. . . . I hope you are well. I know what a poor hand you are at looking after yourself." She knew my mother. Others always came first.

Mother's father owned and ran the Boswell Drug Company in Greenwich. He died before I ever knew him. Will, her half-brother, took over. Her brother Harold lived with his mother and commuted to work in a bank in New York City, starting as a runner. He was an outgoing character, loved to golf, and had a green thumb like his mother. A younger brother had passed away at a very young age.

Mother had trained to be a kindergarten teacher at a seminary in Brooklyn, but we boys were the only recipients of her learning. She was a good-looking brunette with a warm smile. She dressed plainly, spiffier on Sunday for church. She had strong religious roots, and these roots grew deeper as she raised her three sons. She was active in the Second Congregational Church where we went to Sunday school.

We continued to swim at the Rocky Point Club, but the vacation trips to Lake Minnewaska stopped with Dad's death. Buckfield was put on the market and sold, in time to become the site of prestigious backcountry homes in the sophisticated, wealthy Round Hill section of Greenwich. I will always remember the family ties strengthened at Buckfield, and those apple- and blueberry-picking hikes.

Mom could be tough and tart at times. I don't think the hairbrush ever came into play, but I heard "go to your room" some. In our new circumstances, it was fortunate that Mother could drive. It would have been tough otherwise. We used to fight over the rumble seat in the Essex, but now we used Dad's car, which had more room. Mary, the Irish woman hired to help, left after Dad's passing. Mother assumed the full household responsibilities and managed the family finances. I still don't know how she handled it all. I wondered how we switched from coal to oil heat and enclosed the front porch.

She was a fast housekeeper and a good cook. Her homemade root beer (made from a secret formula) is still talked about. She could have put Hires out of business. Now and then a bottle of the tasty brew would blow its cork on the pantry shelf. Her molasses cookies were scrumptious. I recall some of my parents' friends used to come for an occasional seafood feast Mom prepared with my dad's help. The lobsters didn't grab me.

Our Sunday schedule was always Sunday school and then to church as a family. I was a Boy Scout, and we met at the church on Friday nights. It was always a blast, but more so on one particular night when I had a boxing match with a good friend who was bigger and stronger. It didn't look good for me. All of a sudden, with everyone yelling, I flurried a bunch of punches, pounding away at him. He started to bleed and the fight was stopped. The referee raised my arm as the winner. I was really surprised. The result didn't affect our good friendship.

We took a long hike one day and scaled an old stone wall. My foot landed on a copperhead snake. I yelled and jumped away. The scoutmaster responded quickly with an ax.

"Holy cow, here's another one!" I screamed.

My heart pounded, and the ax came down a second time.

One early day in June following Dad's death, Mother took my brother Warner, twelve, and me, eight, by train to

Grand Central Station in New York City. There we joined a bunch of boys headed for Camp Awosting in the same Shawangunk Mountains area near Lake Minnewaska. I am sure Mother felt that we needed more male influences with Dad gone.

I didn't know what to expect, but it turned out to be a ball. I loved the swimming, mountain hiking, and the hours on a tennis court. I learned to handle a canoe, and that was best of all. One night soon after I arrived, though, I had a strange and scary experience.

Taps sounded and the cabin lights went out. It was pitch black, and the only sound came from the peepers in the woods. I had the bunk next to Jim, the counselor. He was a neat fellow, or at least I thought he was. I was tired from tennis, and think I dozed off quickly. I woke suddenly to a hand touching me under the covers. I got scared and sat up quickly. It had to be Jim.

"Jim, what are you doing? Leave me alone."

"Sh-sh-sh."

No answer. I stayed awake for a long time. The next morning I didn't say anything to anyone, including Jim. It never happened again and we were still good friends. He was a good swimming instructor and helped me a lot.

One day a group of us set out on an overnight hike in the mountains with Jim and another counselor. It led to another kind of scare, and the overnight came to a quick end.

It was midafternoon. We were starting to put our tents up when another counselor rushed into our campsite.

"Don't put the tents up. You are all going back to camp now. Move it. Pack up!"

"Why? We just got here. What's going on?" asked Jim.

"Two dangerous convicts have escaped from Nappanoch, the big prison in the valley below. They could be headed this way. Move it. Jim, you take up the rear, and keep them moving."

It was another long hike without stops. We made it back tired, scared, and hungry, but safe and sound. Mother gave me an option to stay another month at Awosting, and I did.

The following summer Mother arranged for me to attend Keewaydin Camps on Lake Dunmore in Vermont. This two-month summer connection continued through my second year in high school. Little did I know how it would influence my future. The lake remains my all-time favorite, sparkling and clean with Mount Moosalamoo providing a stunning backdrop. A great state park with a sandy beach graces its handsome shores.

Canoeing was the specialty at Keewaydin, as it is today. The camp came into being in 1910. The guiding principle was "to build a program so diversified that any boy may derive his own type of satisfaction." The facilities were extensive, the site spectacular, with a combination of valley land, prized lakefront, and a mountain.

My days paddling in a canoe on Adirondack lakes and rivers are memories I will cherish forever. I learned to love life in a wood-and-canvas canoe. I determined to have my own someday as the result of my experiences paddling on Blue Mountain Lake, Long Lake, Tupper Lake, the upper and lower Saranacs, and Raquette Lake and River.

I laugh at one memory. It was an overcast day, the wind was churning up a choppy surface, and the going was rough. We were in a race against ominous storm clouds. We had also bet on who would reach the campsite first. My partner and I quickly fashioned a sail using a ground cloth, a paddle, and rope, and we sailed home first to charges of "foul."

One overnight hiking trip took us to Mount Washington in New Hampshire. The ascent was a steep, rough, and narrow path. Any mention of New England's highest peak brings back that late afternoon "skinny dip" in the Lake of the Clouds. It was like plunging into a big pan of melted ice cubes.

Even after being thrown from a horse and clobbered by a Virginia boy in a boxing ring on Saturday night, I loved my Keewaydin summers. Playing Reuben Corntassel, a country hick, in a camp play was fun and brought laughs. Attending the outdoor memorial service for my friend, Billy, who died of polio, brought tears. I went home to quarantine still thankful to my mother for the Keewaydin days on beautiful Lake Dunmore. My good times there ensured that the outdoors would always be an important part of my life.

Mother transferred me from the public school system to the private Brunswick School for my last three high school years. She was concerned about college preparation. Warner graduated from there, and he was headed for Dartmouth. I could walk to school, and I fared okay in books and extracurricular activities.

At Brunswick I played football in the line with two years on the varsity team. I was light but combative. Once, when clobbered in a rough game, I was carried off the field and revived with smelling salts. Three Skakel brothers were among my friends and teammates. Their sister, Ethel, who became a Kennedy, was a real tomboy. Tennis and track filled out my athletic interests.

I enjoyed playing parts in *Fly Away Home* and Philip Barry's *The Youngest*. The headmaster, who also taught Latin, and my English teacher, the tennis coach, became respected, valuable advisers. Our classes were small, and we received a lot of personal attention.

In my senior year I attended a Pilgrim Fellowship Youth Conference at the University of Connecticut as a delegate from my church. Hundreds attended the lectures and entertainment. It just happened. At a seminar my eyes caught a slim, striking brunette with hair that touched her shoulders.

She was dressed in a white summer dress with a red belt, stockings, and dress heels. She was pretty, had a winning smile, and I couldn't keep my eyes off her. I eased my way toward her.

"What's your name? Where are you from?"

"Tacy — I live in Riverside, go to Greenwich High, and am representing my church in Old Greenwich. How about you?"

"Gosh, what a coincidence. I live in Greenwich, and go to Brunswick School there. I'm here for the Second Congregational Church, the big tall one up on Post Road."

"Have you got sisters and brothers?"

"No sisters. I have an older brother at Dartmouth, and a younger one at home with my mother and me. Our father passed away years ago. How about your family?"

"Dad is a research chemist at a plant in Stamford. We moved here from Massachusetts. I live with my parents and my sister Claire, a few years younger. Got some aunts and uncles, but not around here — Philly and Massachusetts."

The conversations continued as we took long walks on campus, ate together, and got to know each other. There was attraction, but no hot and heavy start on the weekend together.

"Gee, I'm glad I met you. I'll give you a call sometime if that's okay?"

"Sure, I will look forward to it," she said. A warm smile crept over her pretty face.

"I will too." I was in the early throes of a new crush.

I had been dating a number of girls, but never seriously. Movies were my main source of entertainment, occasionally a school dance. I listened to radio for big band music on Martin Block's *Make Believe Ballroom,* and had a record collection. I didn't smoke — I tried cornsilk once — and preferred a Coke to a beer.

My favorite possession during my high school years was a large shortwave radio. It became a hobby that excited and intrigued me. I would retreat to the third-floor attic room and spend hours scanning stations all over the world. I papered the walls with index cards noting the names and locations of the stations I picked up. I heard the bombs drop on Warsaw when the Nazi war machine rolled in, and then Radio Warsaw went dead.

Warner was off at Dartmouth College, and I grew closer to my younger brother, Graham. We threw baseballs, winged footballs, and helped Mother with lawn and garden chores. He was fun, smart, athletic, good looking, and shorter like Dad. He certainly was a joy to Mother, and helped to compensate for the loss of her husband.

Tacy became my steady date. My first visit to her home left me with a favorable impression of her family. Her father was tall, black haired, soft spoken, and friendly. I took an immediate liking to him. Her mother, in contrast, was plain, short, and stocky, perhaps because she was an excellent cook. She was a little talkative. I gathered that she was a homebody — the home was neat and tidy, reflecting her interests — and that she didn't drive a car. Tacy's younger sister, Claire, was pretty, outgoing, and full of fun.

Tacy and I saw a lot of each other on weekends. We went to the movies, took walks, played tennis some, and went to the beach. She was pretty, and the crush became more serious, but it never crossed the line. My family took an immediate liking to her, as I knew they would.

Tacy was already at Colby College in Maine when I chose Washington and Lee University in Virginia as my first choice. One day the headmaster of Brunswick School called me to his office.

"We have just received word that you have been accepted at Washington and Lee University. They did question that mark in Latin, but everything is all set now." The headmaster was my Latin instructor too. Maybe he helped.

"That's neat. That's where I want to go. Thank you, sir."

No doubt my choice had been influenced by a canoe trip at Keewaydin with a former president of the student body at Washington and Lee. The camp director had been a Virginian too. I was thrilled and couldn't wait to get home to tell my mother.

The reputation and size of the university and the community pleased me, although I had never been there. Going to college in Virginia would be an education in a new environment, but I did think that my girl in Maine might be disappointed with the increased distance.

I was one of thirteen in the thirty-ninth Brunswick graduating class in 1941. The founder and original headmaster spoke: "Twenty years ago many said that there were no frontiers left. How things have changed. The world we knew has been shattered. . . . No intelligent man believes that when the world has been pieced together that it will be anything like it has been in the past.

"The country and world have set new frontiers. The world is waiting to be made over. The job is yours. The job will never be complete. The will to win will make you free."

College and War

*Such happiness as life is capable of comes from the full
participation of all our powers in the endeavor to
wrest from each changing situation of experience its
own full and unique meaning.*

JOHN DEWEY

Mother was enthusiastic about my choice of college in Virginia and also about the trip to get me there. Warner had transferred to Columbia University, intent on journalism. Graham was in public grade school. She arranged to drive me down.

Mother's travel had been limited to nearby New England, vacations at Lake Minnewaska in New York, and an occasional trip to the Poconos in Pennsylvania where Dad and she enjoyed playing golf.

Dad and Mom were married in 1914, and her diary describes their wedding and honeymoon without romantic overtones, but Mother was a private person in many ways. Her daily diary entries usually ended with "Stan came over." That was it.

Saturday, June 27, 1914
Busy as a bee — helped decorate, made punch, etc.

— Bessie came — had lunch — helped around —
Stan came over — fussed — Gladys fixed veil — got
dressed for wedding — married at six-thirty —
received — ate — changed clothes — went amid
showers of confetti to Tarrytown (Florence Inn) in
machine — picked up confetti — talked, etc. — bed.

Her diary comments on the honeymoon trip that followed and described

the train to Poughkeepsie — boat to Albany —
train to Saratoga Springs — train to Lake George
— a trolley back to Saratoga — train to Pittsfield
— train to Stamford home.

Otherwise it was

talked — took walks — dinner — went to bed.

Her diary comments were short and matter of fact. They
didn't reveal her deep feelings, but she had them, and they
grew. Below each daily diary entry was a quotation, a poem,
a Bible verse, or a few lines in her own handwriting that
revealed her feelings, like this one:

Let us learn to be content with what we have. Let
us get rid of our false estimates. Set up all the
higher ideals: a quiet home, vines of our own
planting, a few books full of the inspiration of
genius, a few friends worthy of being loved and able
to love us in return, a hundred pleasures that bring
us no pain or sorrow, a devotion to the right that
will never swerve, a simple religion empty of all
bigotry, full of trust and hope and love — and to

such a philosophy this world will give up all the
empty joy it has.

DAVID SWING

It describes her feelings and embodies her conduct. Her code
made her strong: to live modestly, quietly, and to be ever
growing.

It was a beautiful sunny day when we crossed the
Mason-Dixon line and entered the South for the first time.
We made good time, Mother's heavy foot on the gas pedal
contributing. We checked in to a hotel in Washington D.C.
a few blocks from the capitol. Time was limited for any sight-
seeing, but we gained entrance to the capitol for a short tour
including its rotunda.

"I've always wanted to come here, and now I have," she
said.

"This is a first for both of us, Mom."

"Your dad had two years in the capitol at Hartford when
he was a legislator, but we never made it here."

"Was he a good politician? Did he like it?"

"I don't know about politician. He got elected. People
liked him. All I know is that your dad was hardworking,
honest, fair, and caring. He took his responsibilities as a judge
and a legislator very seriously. I think he enjoyed it most of
the time."

"It took a lot of his time, didn't it?"

"Yes, it did, but we managed. As a lawyer he was constantly dealing with his clients' problems, and in the legisla-
ture with public issues. If he had lived, Lord knows what he
might have become."

The next morning we only had time for a brief stop at
the Lincoln Memorial. We stood together and read the
Gettysburg Address inscribed on the wall. Mother was especially touched. A few tears came to her eyes. Maybe her

thoughts had turned again to Dad. I believe they often did.

We caught a first glimpse of the Washington and Lee campus, and to this day the image remains indelible. It is among my favorite places, and always will be. There is nothing more relaxing for me than walking the colonnade on this spectacular and historical campus, just steps from where Robert E. Lee rests. We were also impressed with picturesque Lexington and its many historical gems.

My roommate, Linwood, was from tiny Big Stone Gap in the coal country of southwestern Virginia. His hair was red, his face ruddy. Linwood was friendly and outgoing. I sensed we would hit it off just fine. I didn't know then this likable country guy was destined to become the first Republican governor of Virginia in one hundred years, and a good one.

The next morning I turned to my mother. "Mom, thanks for everything you have done to make this possible, and for getting me here. I like what I see. I'll do okay." I gave her a hug and kissed her. I was concerned about her long trip back, but I honestly don't think she gave it a thought. Her faith was unlimited, and He would be with her all the way.

My New England accent was a dead giveaway that I was from the North, and I had to get accustomed to some deep Southern ones. I was immediately surprised and perplexed by the status of black citizens in the area. They went to the rear of the bus to ride, and could only occupy the last few rows in the balcony at the State Theatre. Some stepped off the sidewalk to let you pass. I felt sorry for them. It wasn't right.

I was enchanted with my new environment. I read a lot about Robert E. Lee, and now he became my real hero. He combined the characteristics of a Southern gentleman with a warm human being; he was a great commanding general, and became a dedicated, visionary educator. The oratorical elegance of Dr. Francis P. Gaines, Washington and Lee's

Washington and Lee University

president, only reinforced my respect for the gray soldier with the white beard. I often imagined Lee walking the white pillared colonnade on front campus, a magnetic and peaceful scene of sheer beauty.

Lee Chapel is captivating with its white-pillared balconies on either side above the main floor with its two red-carpeted aisles. The white marble recumbent statue of Lee, depicting rest on a battlefield, looms behind the attractive front platform, and draws immediate attention. A few historic oil paintings catch a wandering eye. A simple plaque notes the pew seat that Lee regularly occupied as college president. I couldn't resist sitting there for a few reflective moments.

Douglas Southall Freeman, the noted historian of Lee, describes the man as "simple and spiritual." Lee's own moral code lives in words he penned on a battlefield in the Civil War:

The forebearing use of power does not only form a
touchstone, but the manner in which an individual
enjoys certain advantages over others is a test of a
true gentleman.

The power which the strong have over the
weak, the employer over the employees, the educated over the unlettered, the experienced over the
confiding, even the clever over the silly — the
forbearing or inoffensive use of all this power or
authority or a total abstinence from it when the
case admits it, will show the gentleman in plain
light. The gentleman does not needlessly and
unnecessarily remind an offender of a wrong he
may have committed against him. He cannot only
forgive, he can forget; and he strives for that noble-
ness of self and mildness of character which impart
sufficient strength to let the past be the past. A true
man of honor feels humbled himself when he
cannot help humbling others.

The days that unfolded were happy ones. I believe my
education was enhanced by real Southern exposure. The
classes were small, and the professors displayed close personal interest in my progress. The coats and ties of Southern gentlemen were required unless the professor became
overheated in class. An honor code, established under Lee,
prevailed on campus.

I became active in intramural sports and extracurricular
activities including the campus paper and magazine. Joining a fraternity hyped my social life. I had difficulty climbing ropes to the ceiling in gym class. I plunged into Latin
again and was shocked to win a scholarship in it.

During my free time I saw Rosalie at a nearby college
for women. I remember a cold, winter's night ride in an open

car trunk over the Blue Ridge Mountains to see her. It was worth it. She was a trim, natural Southern beauty who helped to make life interesting at dances, football games, and the movies. I thought of my girl up North, but presumed she was dating too.

I was in my dormitory room on Sunday afternoon, December 7, 1941. The radio brought the news of the Japanese bombing of Pearl Harbor. We all spent the day by our radios and listened to the war news. When the strains of the *Star Spangled Banner* pealed forth the dormitory echoed with the sound of everyone singing. We all listened intently to the president's address, and stood and cheered him at the conclusion. A lot of guys wanted to enlist.

I thought to myself that a lowering of the draft age was inevitable. The radio was bubbling with chatter about this happening soon. I was sure my college career would be interrupted. It was bound to be. Everyone twenty-one, registered or not, was asked to fill out a form. I figured it wouldn't be long now.

It was harder to study knowing that my college days were numbered. I had seriously considered the ministry at one point. A high school classmate and I soon made a trip to New York City for personal contact with the American Field Service about ambulance driving. We were informed they wanted men ready for immediate departure for Egypt. That ended that.

It was volunteer or wait to be drafted. I chose to enlist in the Army Reserves, gain some deferment, and await the inevitable. I went to the basement of Doremus Gymnasium on campus to take the necessary steps.

"Young man, are you getting enough to eat? We need some more skin on your bones to let you in the army. You're underweight."

"How much? What can I do? I'm in sports and I'm healthy," I said.

"Tell you what you can do," replied the young lieutenant. "You go and start drinking milkshakes and eating bananas — all you can. You come back late tomorrow or the next morning. We'll still be here, and you just might make it. How's that sound?"

"Okay, I'll be here," and I was the next day. I made it by the skin of my teeth.

"Any problem, young man?"

"No, sir, not really — just in my stomach, and that's disposable."

I thanked the sympathetic officer, and took off for the nearest men's room. I figured latrines would soon be next.

A few months later Tacy flew down from Maine to attend the fancy dress ball with me. It was good to see her and I wondered when I would see her next. She was a hit with my fraternity brothers. We danced the night away to the big band sounds of Harry James. I suspected it was a last fling. Again we didn't take things to any serious extreme — just had a great weekend.

Books and I ended our close association in January 1943, and I requested active duty. I enjoyed some limited time at home with family, Tacy, and friends. I left for Fort Devens, Massachusetts, on a cold Valentine's Day along with a high school classmate, Bob. Together we stepped into the unknown, like many others who had gone before us.

With medical checks, some instruction, KP, and latrine duty over it was off to wet and dreary Sea Girt on the Jersey coast for basic training and tests. Fort Monmouth nearby was the next stop for training as a high-speed radio operator, and mastering Morse code. I was selected to enter the Army Specialized Training Program. Several weeks of orientation and tests followed at the City College of New York. Next I found myself in Hannibal Hamlin Hall on the campus of the University of Maine, back in classrooms. Science courses, no friends of mine, were the basic curriculum.

I was pleased that some English and speech courses were finally woven into the offerings — more my speed. I attended church in town most Sundays. I took an interesting tour of the Old Town Canoe Company nearby where artisans of Native American heritage created handsome wood-and-canvas canoes with sleek mahogany gunnels. It recalled canoe trip days at Keewaydin in Vermont, and I renewed my determination to own a canoe someday.

One day in June four hundred of us were required to undergo physical fitness tests on the football field. An officer barked out: "Get in position and lie on your back with your hands clasped behind your head. On the count of *one* raise your body and touch the left elbow to your right knee. On *two* return to position. On *three* raise and touch the right elbow to left knee. On *four* return to position, hands behind your head."

Thirty-two times was deemed acceptable. Many floundered. I kept on going when all the rest were done in. They crowded around to watch as I repeated the exercise one hundred and one times. The army had me in good shape at 157 pounds. That chow? Maybe the milkshakes off duty. I thought of that day the Army Reserves first rejected me.

It was strange. Here I was in Maine where Tacy had first gone to college. She had transferred to the University of Connecticut to be nearer to home and me when I was stationed in New Jersey. It didn't work.

On a subzero day in February 1944 many of us received news that we would depart immediately for new destinations. My orders were to report back to Fort Monmouth, New Jersey. I arrived in New York City with an overnight pass and slept on an elderly aunt's couch.

The next morning I went to Pennsylvania Station where

I purchased a copy of the *New York Daily News*. There, on the front page, was a picture and the story of a tragic fire that had consumed Hannibal Hamlin Hall on the University of Maine campus. There had been deaths in the third-floor section I had just left.

My God. I couldn't believe it. I would have been there if it weren't for the timing of my orders. I was shocked. I realized how lucky I was — how unlucky some others were. It was upsetting news.

Stepped-up classroom and field training as a high-speed radio operator came next. There was a taste of combat conditions too. I remember the live bullets from a machine gun whizzing over me as I squirmed through a muddy course. I uncovered and diffused a land mine with some hesitancy. I ran down a narrow path, grabbed a dangling rope, and swung out over a brook. Damned if I didn't make it, on my feet, to the other side. A green lieutenant followed me, and plopped midstream. I chuckled quietly with a little glee at his unexpected bath in cold water. All in all, I figured our days were numbered now.

A strong hint came a few days later when a small group of us, with our captain, were loaded on to a bus in late afternoon. The destination turned out to be Joe King's Fraternity House, at the corner of Seventeenth Street and Third Avenue in New York City. Lots of cold beer mixed with steak, stories, emotions, and a few pretty women. Good friends mixed loud fun moments with serious quiet ones. We all contemplated the near future.

A night later there was a USO send-off show at the Post Theatre. We rose in the foggy darkness the next morning and with full gear got on to a crammed troop train that had all the shades drawn. We were logically headed west. The general atmosphere was subdued. Some read, some dozed, and some just sat with their thoughts.

The final stop turned out to be Seattle, Washington. No real surprise. We disembarked, and spent about two weeks at Fort Lewis in final preparation for whatever was ahead. I really didn't give the future much thought. How could any of us?

It was pitch black in early morning when I drove the jeep through downtown Seattle streets to the docks and the USS *Patrick*. Its decks were crammed with combat-ready GIs, and more were boarding. Antiaircraft guns caught my eye. I was in awe as we passed under a bridge in Puget Sound and I caught my first glimpse of the endless, blue Pacific.

My first duty was assigned quickly. On deck, with eyes straight ahead, I strained to detect signs of any enemy subs. Others, at intervals, did the same. Rumor had it we were being shadowed, but others speculated we could outrun them. There was no visible air cover.

That night I tossed and turned on my bunk in the crowded belly of the ship. Only someone's occasional snore or cough broke the strange silence. It was hot, and all kinds of thoughts arose. I really didn't have any feel for danger ahead, but all of a sudden war was real. The big question: where were we headed?

I found out when Diamond Head loomed into view. The run to Oahu, Hawaii, was without incident. A small contingent of high-speed radio operators was ordered to disembark, and I was surprised to find myself one of the lucky ones.

We headed inland in trucks, and I caught my first look at the interior beyond the long, inviting beaches. I noted the heavy presence of army and navy personnel. There were endless pineapple fields; some deep, red-clay valleys; flowery jungle terrain; and lush, cloud-scraping mountains. Someone pointed out a cut in the mountains where Japanese planes had winged in to bomb Pearl Harbor. I was thankful to be late on the scene.

My thoughts kept returning to guys on the ship, wondering if it had pulled out, and where it was going. Rumors circulated that it was headed for Okinawa.

The trip through pineapple fields ended with a cluster of barracks, and duty commenced in an underground communications center. I was a high-speed, fixed-station radio operator but switched to handling high-speed, tape-relay stations all over the world. I soon obtained cryptographic clearance as well. I was aware of Japanese intercept facilities.

I came to love Oahu, its mix of people, the climate, and certainly the swimming. After night shifts I often slept on a beach. How I got there is another story.

Soon after my arrival I was talked into a hundred-dollar, one-third ownership of a 1931 Hupmobile with a rumble seat. I was told that the rear tires were from a Grumman Hellcat airplane. I never probed the origin, but they did give a distinct lean to the vehicle. Days later I inherited full ownership at a reduced price when the other two owners had to ship out.

The test ride was unusual. We were enroute to a barefoot, high school football game in Honolulu. The car lurched unexpectedly, the front end dropped, and the left front wheel went off down a long hill. An oncoming jeep veered to miss it. We found the wheel, remounted it, and, a little late, enjoyed the game.

The car more than paid for itself. I charged fifty cents for off-duty runs to and from a stunning beach. I had no problem finding passengers.

One day I drove the car to the top of Pali Pass. It was a bright, sunny day with a heavy breeze. I parked and took in the spectacular view below. A naval officer in a jeep pulled alongside and struck up a conversation.

"They tell me that winds have been so heavy up here they have blown a few jeeps into the valley."

"Think you're safe today, and I don't think my rumble-seat tank would fly like your jeep," I replied.

"I hear there are some places on the island where Jap parachutes still dangle in some inaccessible locations. Seen any?" he said.

"No, but I have heard that."

It was a lousy night to have guard duty. Slow-moving storm clouds were dumping buckets of rain on the complex of buildings. I splashed through the puddles, and heaved a sigh of relief as it let up. I detected a sound and saw a figure near the corner of a building. It disappeared. I repeatedly challenged, "Who goes there?" No response. I winged off a single shot from my M1 high to the corner of the building. It produced a quick and anxious response from an overachieving second lieutenant. "Just checking."

That was all, and that was that.

I know how lucky I was to have been stationed in Hawaii. I thought of those who kept going on that crowded troopship to whatever destination. Being stationed in Hawaii was hardly "overseas duty," but it was essential duty in that important communications center.

One night I took an incoming tape-relay message that said it all. "YF Relay — The War Is Over — WAR." Some exuberant operator at the War Department sent this unofficial clear text about the Japanese capitulation. Pandemonium broke loose, and thoughts naturally turned to home. Mine sure did.

Later that night I talked with some Mormon friends in my barracks and for some reason the conversation turned to Vermont. Ken and the others were great friends. I never really got into their religious views and they didn't push me. I was impressed with their personal standards, their work ethic, their caring and intelligence. I did recall that Joseph

Smith, the American founder of the Mormon Church, made the trek with his followers to Utah from Vermont.

One morning months later, in February 1946, the word came. "You're shipping out — going home. You go for embarkation tomorrow morning. Pack up."

"Oh, my gosh — the car!" I panicked.

Late that afternoon I slipped out of camp in the Hupmobile headed for a native village across the pineapple fields. My heart was in my throat. My aging pal had just lost one forward gear. A crowd circled the vehicle in the village center. Competition produced quick cash. I hightailed it on foot back to camp in record time, much relieved and well compensated.

Early the next morning, as a staff sergeant, I was transported to the embarkation point. The following day I boarded the Matson liner SS *Lurline* for San Francisco, headed for discharge and then home. Conversation, laughter, music, and song resonated on the happy, crowded decks. It was a complete contrast to my first experience on a troopship.

Some stood silently at the railings, gazing at the far horizon adrift in their own sea of thoughts. I joined them looking eastward. My brother Warner was already back home in civilian clothes after seeing plenty of action in Europe and slugging his way into Germany. His letters home certainly contrasted with mine. His earlier service in California led to marriage to a tall, dark-haired beauty from Colorado — as nice as she looked.

Mother had done volunteer work during the war's earlier days: she spotted for enemy intrusions into Long Island Sound from a wooden tower on the Connecticut shoreline. She also spent hours a week making surgical dressings at her church. Although Mother never let grass grow under her feet, I was well aware that she was always penning caring letters to her sons.

Graham, my younger brother, now in his early teens, was at home and I couldn't wait to see him. I am sure he was still the great consolation for Mom and a willing helper.

I mulled over a return to college in Virginia under the GI bill. A career choice was still up in the air, but law seemed uppermost in my mind. My major thoughts revolved around my girl, who was wearing my engagement ring. We had not seen each other in a long time. Her letters had been steady and recently had dwelled heavily on wedding plans. I honestly didn't give them much thought, knowing it would be awhile. All I knew now was that I was going home. It was a good feeling. I was unsettled. I was certainly more mature, just not too sure of anything. The stimulating Pacific air and blue waters brought a calm to my muddled mind. I turned and sacked out on the deck.

The sight of San Francisco was welcome, even Alcatraz. It was off to Camp Stoneman, then on to Camp Beale for final paperwork, discharge, and a return to civilian life on Valentine's Day 1946. I took the train home to Connecticut wearing a loud blue Hawaiian shirt. The army paid my fare. The spectacular mountain scenes in the Rockies left me in wondrous reverence. The flat stretches midcountry were a disappointing contrast, and I longed for New England again.

My heart beat a little faster as the train slowed for its stop in Stamford. I grabbed my bag and got off. There they were — my mother and my girl — the women whose letters had filled the past three years. I flung my arms around them both, kissed them, and said, "I'm back." I felt a lump in my throat and held back tears. It dawned on me once again how lucky I was to really be home. What now?

t h r e e

The Return

*If, almost on the day of their landings, our ancestors
founded schools and colleges, what obligations do
rest upon us, living under circumstances more
favorable, both for providing and using the means
of education?*

DANIEL WEBSTER

My relationship with Tacy gained new life after my long absence. She was wrapped up in wedding plans. I focused on my stepped-up summer return to college and finding an apartment. Inwardly I harbored a few thoughts that I needed more time before taking that walk down a church aisle. There wasn't much time to sort it all out. If we both went to Lexington we would have to be married.

I remember one night of hesitation and skepticism. On the spur of the moment I contacted Jean, my first real girl-friend from grade school days. We went to the movies, then sat for a long time talking and reminiscing in Bruce Park. Our hands touched, but nothing else. It helped, but only added food for thought.

A few days later Claire and I were sitting in my car in the driveway waiting for Tacy. The wedding plans came up.

"Getting nervous about the big day?" she asked.

"Yes, too many arrangements and fancy details."

"It will be all over soon . . . hang in."

"Gee, maybe I'm marrying the wrong sister," I said half jokingly to my friend, the maid of honor. It brought a smile, and then Tacy appeared. The conversation ended.

The May 11 wedding date loomed, and the mounting preparations flustered me some. I just rolled with them. I was buoyed by the prospect of two army buddies coming to be ushers. I was in love, but concerned about the responsibilities that lay ahead.

The wedding took place in the Second Congregational Church. One newspaper noted the wedding as "the first lavish one of the season in Greenwich." I was very embarrassed by the write-up, typically wealthy Greenwich. I would have much preferred something more low key, less glossy. Then again it wasn't my decision. A reception at a nearby yacht club crowned the occasion. Deep down I had already made up my mind never to live there or to commute to New York for work. It just wasn't my world. I had changed.

We went to the Chateau Frontenac in Quebec City in my mother's car on our honeymoon. It was like a cheap visit to France without crossing the ocean. I remember the fancy, foiled chocolates on the pillows and the sweet night that followed. We relaxed on a carriage ride, walked the quaint streets, and grew closer in the days and nights that followed. We did experience some trouble with the car, but not the honeymoon.

Soon after our return to Greenwich there was a welcome call from Lexington and I ran to tell Tacy.

"We have the apartment. It's on the second floor. It's pretty well furnished — large bedroom, living room, and well-equipped kitchen, some closets, lots of windows. It's in an older home on South Main Street — a nice area. It's just a short walk to the campus and downtown."

"What about the rent? Heated?" she asked.

"It's okay — right on the money. There will be four other students and their wives in the place too. I remember the house — has some old slave quarters out back."

The trip to Lexington for the start of summer school went smoothly. The apartment's rooms were large and pleasant. We added some large rugs and a few curtains. I plunged into books and planned to combine my senior year of undergraduate work with first-year law school. I decided to become a lawyer with the help of the GI bill. Tacy found enjoyable work in a gift shop just off campus.

We later moved to new government housing units opposite my fraternity house for returning veteran couples. We gained a social advantage from that, and also an additional bedroom.

The torrid summer heat was not conducive to long hours of studying. I began to think about changing my career objective. I wanted to move more quickly out into the work world. I shared my feelings with my wife under a shade tree.

"I've made the decision to withdraw from law school, change some courses, and speed graduation with a Bachelor of Arts."

"Why? What will you do?" she asked.

"I don't think I want to take on the daily problems of others as a lawyer. I have in mind going into radio broadcasting — it's timely. If not, maybe hotel management. I have given it a lot of thought," I answered.

"Of course I want you to do what you think is best," she added. She was helpful.

"The heat, the books, the timing, the responsibilities, money . . . I have considered them all. I think I should go for the change."

I changed my courses and studied hard the summer of 1947 to speed my exit.

I was relieved and relaxed when I entered the handsome office of the president late in the morning of September 4. President Gaines and Dean of Students Gilliam were present. I was greeted warmly. The latter knew every student by his first name.

"Good morning, Dean. We know this is an important day for you and that these surroundings are not our normal scene for conferring degrees, but these are unusual times," said the president.

"I feel this place is just the right place, sir — devoid of pomp and circumstance — no cap or hot gown, no long procession or speeches, and it's nice and cool. I couldn't have better commencement speakers either," I replied.

There was a ripple of laughter, and then I received brief, timely, reassuring words from two admired and respected gentlemen at my "private" graduation ceremony in historic Washington Hall. I thanked them, shook hands, and left to take one last walk along that famous colonnade — that B.A. certificate tucked under my arm.

I felt strangely sad to be leaving the campus I loved. I felt confident about my ability to face the future having been nurtured by the total Washington and Lee experience. Could it be that I also acquired a little "rebel" sense too?

My thoughts turned to commercial radio broadcasting, probably stimulated by my communications work in the service. I also gave some fleeting thoughts to gaining a foothold in hotel management.

My wife continued to work at the Dutch Inn while I initiated a job search in Virginia. I took a bus to Covington to audition for an announcer position. It didn't work out. I shifted my sights higher, and nervously auditioned at WROV, Roanoke. It included a cemetery commercial and led to a dead end. Things didn't look so good. Maybe I was barking up the wrong tree.

I gained an appointment at a major station in Arlington, WEAM, but sensed I was out of my league. Jerry Strong, a top D.C. air personality, auditioned me. After the audition Jerry, joined by the general manager, Mr. Brown, offered me counsel.

"You read well, but the voice — New England, isn't it? — will hamper you in finding an announcing position. Maybe in a small town radio station, probably not beyond," Jerry said.

"I already sense that," I said.

"Young man, I would like to suggest you consider other ways of securing good employment in the broadcast field — accounting, writing copy, news, sales, and engineering. Radio is a great field right now, and the timing is right," Mr. Brown said.

"Not engineering I'm sure, sir. . . . I really appreciate the time and advice you both have given me."

The conversation continued at length and I listened to them intently. Their attitude and wise counsel made a significant impact. I thanked them for their courtesy and help. I left relaxed and upbeat, determined to incorporate their courtesy, standards, and practice in my own future endeavors. People can make a difference when they go out of their way to help others.

A week later, acting on a lead, I arrived at the Tides Inn in Gloucester, near the coast, and applied for hotel work. Tacy accompanied me. The visit didn't supply a job but did provide a good tip. We sped on to the famous Williamsburg Inn and Lodge. The next morning I received an offer to train in their renowned food and dining enterprises. My wife was offered work in their gift shop. We took the evening to make the decision and lingered on it. The next morning, with thanks, we said no. We did think about the results of a yes.

Tacy and I went back to Lexington, and then left for Greenwich. My search now turned to Vermont, and it was helped by my grandmother's graduation gift of a new two-door Chevrolet.

Leaving Tacy at home with her parents, I drove to Vermont, the state I had come to love so much in earlier days. I felt I was headed in the right direction at last and only hoped I could find a good job in radio. There were only a few radio stations in the entire state. I decided to begin my search in Burlington, on Lake Champlain, the largest populated area.

I passed the old Brandon Inn where I remember, as a youngster, flinging lighted firecrackers out a window. I caught the devil for it from my mother and grandparents. I detoured to swing around Lake Dunmore where I had spent so many happy days at Keewaydin as a camper. I gazed up at the cloudy shroud hovering over Rattlesnake Point on Mount Moosalamoo where I used to hike. I parked the car, took a long drink of cold water from the old hand-pumped artesian well nearby, and started a leisurely stroll through the entire camp.

Many names and faces came to mind as I wandered along the quiet shoreline, including Jeff Smith, a minister and old-time staff member, notable for having a hole in his head that had been inflicted by a real tiger. H. P. McCarthy, the genial, bald Irish camp counselor came to mind when I passed our old tent platform.

I drove to nearby Branbury Beach on the lake. I took off my shoes and walked the shoreline, the soft sand crunching between the toes on my burning feet. I sipped on a can of Coke, deep in thought. I needed to find a job quickly. Mother and Uncle Sam put me through college. Now I was on my own — not quite. I had a wife to care for too — and no job. Why didn't I wait awhile?

I returned to the car and headed for Burlington. Off to

the west the Adirondack Mountains of New York filled the horizon. Lake Champlain was in the foreground, basking in the late afternoon sun. It was a memorable return to the Green Mountain state. I felt at home and only hoped I could find the means to stay.

The next morning my hopes rose when I was surprisingly offered a position opening in thirty days at the major radio station, C. P. Hasbrook's WCAX — not as an announcer. I was impressed by the professional courtesy extended to me and by what I saw. It was the top radio station in the state.

The only real drawback was the thirty-day wait. I didn't commit right off and drove on to Montpelier, the state capital, to follow up on a lead that a radio station was in the offing. That old adage came to mind — "nothing ventured, nothing gained." My confidence was pumped up.

The hour drive to the smallest state capital was scenic, and I spotted Camels Hump towering in the maze of Green Mountains to the south. The shiny gold dome of the state capitol captured my eyes as I drove slowly down the main street into the heart of the city, no larger than Lexington, Virginia.

I placed a quick phone call and connected with two young men from Iowa in the process of building a radio station in Montpelier. I climbed the creaky stairs to the third floor of an old red-brick building on a downtown corner to meet with Bernie and Carl, the owners. The modest office area, studio, and control room were almost complete. Both individuals made a good impression. We talked at great length. They described a staff position still open, with an immediate start date. That raised my interest.

"The job covers a number of areas. In essence you will be the assistant business manager handling bookkeeping for client accounts, payroll, and the like. Our CPA will orient you, and provide what help you may need at the outset," said Carl.

"I believe I can handle that," I said.

"Wait, there's more to it. You will also be in charge of traffic. By that I mean you would handle the paperwork enabling you to produce a precise and printed daily program log. This reflects program names and times with sponsor identification. Similarly it does the same for one-minute and thirty-second announcements throughout the broadcast day. You'll receive the information from the program director, and by time-order forms from the sales staff. We have hired someone who will write our commercial copy for client ads, but she may need help now and then."

"I'd like that. I like to write," I said.

"You could get your feet wet in sales too, here in the office at least. Our sales staff will be out pounding. You'll know our advertising rates for both announcements and programs."

"Okay. I'd like that. I believe I can sell."

The conversation quickly turned to hours, pay, and a starting date. The salary offered was minimal and I expected the hours would be long, particularly at the outset while I was learning. The conversation never touched on announcing and that was fine. The offer provided an entry key, and the chance to gain on-the-job training and experience in a number of areas. I was in luck.

"Well, the job is yours if you want to give it a shot," said Carl with Bernie chiming in.

"I'll take it, and do my best. When do you want me to start?"

"Tomorrow. You can help us unload the transmitter and some other equipment at the transmitter shack and tower site on the edge of the city, and we'll go on from there."

My first job in radio — at WSKI — was a reality. I left

the interview to find a room in a private home. In high spir-its I called my wife. "I have a job, and will look for an apart-ment right off so you can join me." I gave her some details. A week or so later I found a nice second-floor apartment a few blocks from the shiny dome of the capitol. I was re-lieved and upbeat and I felt at home back in Vermont.

Tacy's father soon delivered her to Montpelier, and we made the welcome move to the apartment. She quickly found work as a receptionist with an insurance company in the same office building where I worked. I was energized and took ev-ery opportunity I could to learn about the radio business. John, the CPA, was particularly helpful on the business end.

I found Vermonters outgoing and friendly right from the start. I had been forewarned that they were aloof, inde-pendent, and wary of newcomers in their midst. My wife and I were pleasantly surprised and felt right at home.

Winter in Vermont was a new experience with heaps of snow and consistent cold, even subzero temperatures. The air was dry and brisk — made you feel good, properly clothed. The heavy snows turned the mountain scenery into a capti-vating wonderland. I marveled at how efficiently the plows cleared the roads, and how few school makeup days occurred.

My enthusiasm for radio soared and one night singer Rosemary Clooney helped. I was designated to shuttle her from Barre to Montpelier for a concert appearance, and back. It was just the two of us. Wow, to be so lucky. I was an immediate fan of the person as well as the singer.

It was late in the evening when I finished some work at the station. Jim, the chief engineer, was wrapping up some work on a tape recorder.

"Dean, let's go get a cup of coffee."

"Okay with me. I'm ready."

The conversation over coffee turned to a lengthy talk about radio and our dreams.

"You know, Jim, I would love to have my own radio station someday," I said. "I've got the bug, not the experience, not the money — just the dream. I don't know a darn thing about the engineering side you know, and that's essential."

"I've got some radio engineering experience around a few stations. I'd like nothing better than to get into ownership and build a station . . . but I sure as hell don't know where I'd get the money either," replied Jim. We talked for about an hour.

Conversations about our mutual dream continued in the days ahead. We talked about where we could build one in Vermont and what frequencies were open. Jim did some checking. I wrote the Federal Communications Commission for information and to see what the application forms entailed. We did some checking on what it would take to make the dream come true.

In mid-1947 fate stepped in when I received an unexpected gift of ten thousand dollars from my grandfather. I shared the information first with my wife, and then with Jim. We had the possibility of making our dream come true, and I set the windfall aside for that purpose. I was determined to make it pay off.

We shifted into high gear, teamed our limited experience, plotted, and planned. Brazenly we decided to apply for a full-time AM radio station in St. Johnsbury, located in the northeast section of the state, which was presently without a station.

In the weeks that followed we burned the roads to St. Johnsbury in off-hours. We connected with John, a local attorney. We made contacts with some professional civic-minded and business leaders, explaining our plan. There was encouragement, and we initiated a successful drive to sell stock at ten dollars a share to augment our limited resources. John received stock in return for his legal services at the outset.

Members of my family were concerned at my leap, pointing out that I had no real experience. That mother of mine stood by me again and bought some limited shares for herself and also in the name of each brother. Marbles, my dad's former secretary, did the same. Her sister, Marie, bought more. The family purchases cemented my already majority ownership.

Tacy was supportive as I worked evenings to prepare and submit an application to the Federal Communications Commission. It was filed by Earl, an attorney in a Washington law firm specializing in communications. I was concerned about the limited financial resources reflected and crossed my fingers.

Jim and I broke the news where we worked, resigned, and made arrangements to move to St. Johnsbury to find a site, advance our plans, and hopefully wait out government approval.

Tacy and I were immediately impressed with St. Johnsbury. Its wide shaded Main Street was lined with unique and ornate homes and buildings in Victorian dress. Large green lawns and colorful flower beds added trim. The imposing Athanaeum and Art Gallery, the Fairbanks Museum and Planetarium, and the huge stone North Congregational Church towered over the attractive "plain."

Down the street we noted the attractive brick buildings of St. Johnsbury Academy, a private school serving as the town's public high school, and nearby a courthouse from another day. Calvin Coolidge, a Vermonter and the country's thirtieth president, had attended the school in 1891 as a postgraduate student before entering Amherst College. I learned that all these larger eye-catching gems were among the gifts of the Fairbanks family, inventors of the first platform scale, and the largest employer in the area.

The downtown business area had some of the same Victorian facades and seemed busy. Train service at the railroad station was only a one-train remnant of its heyday in the mid-1880s. There were numerous residential areas, mostly old, mostly neat, some new.

A few miles out of town was a countryside of rolling hills and, in the distance, lofty mountain peaks scratching the sky. I liked what I saw. St. Johnsbury is the major town in the three-county area called the Northeast Kingdom, a name bestowed by its revered U.S. senator, George D. Aiken. It is still the most rural area in Vermont, replete with scenic communities and church spires, farms, lakes, rivers, and brooks. Vast wilderness areas join to mix with the background of mountain magic. I was hooked.

We found a second-floor apartment with a sizable front porch overlooking a park near the academy. It was satisfactory and you could easily walk to town. That helped Tacy, who didn't have a driver's license.

The search for a radio station site began in earnest. It ended in an eleven-acre pasture atop a hill with a barn cellar hole, lined on three sides with stone walls. The needed utilities were available at the edge of a developing residential area. It was a real find at a welcome price.

We gambled and bought the land. We gambled again and bought a ten-year-old tower in Savannah, Georgia, to be dismantled and shipped. That would be a problem if our application was turned down. Tacy found work at the local Ralston Purina Company as a receptionist-secretary. I obtained a humdrum position with the St. Johnsbury Trucking Company, shuffling shipping orders by day.

Earl, our Washington attorney, said that only time was holding up favorable approval. We decided to construct a building on the cellar hole to house station operations. Jim and I spent all our free time, evenings and weekends, doing actual construction after some major initial work had been completed by our contractor. We dug the long water and sewer trenches by hand. We put roof rafters in place, studded and wallboarded rooms. We hung doors and painted. Jim did the bulk of the electrical work and installed the first radiant glass heating panels in the area.

In a real economy measure we stapled Sears egg-crate carton dividers to the walls and ceilings of the control room for acoustic control. Maybe Vermont ingenuity and thrift were catching on. The cost was eight dollars and fifty cents. We cleaned, washed windows, and helped to lay tile. We sweated and waited and waited for government approval as we began to put the staff at least in focus. That's all we could do.

Jim and I would be comanagers. He would oversee the engineering, technical equipment, and help on general programming. I would handle the business and sales end with input on programming too. The corporate structure was finalized for Twin State Broadcasters, Inc., the owner-applicant. As majority stockholder I was the president and treasurer, and Jim was vice president.

Tacy and I quickly felt at home in St. Johnsbury. We found our neighbors friendly and helpful. She liked her work and the people she worked with. She rolled with my stress in good humor. The thought of starting a family wasn't even a current topic of conversation. It was certainly not the time.

After initial skepticism, my family was intrigued with my plunge into broadcasting and I was thankful for their encouragement. It meant a lot. Deep down I felt that the time was ripe and the place was right. I guessed that the publisher and editor of the family-owned daily newspaper, which dated back to 1837, would have other feelings. I didn't expect their warm welcome, but I was sure there was room for both media.

Jim's spirit and mine suffered from application approval delay. Sorting those shipping orders at the trucking company became a more boring struggle. Jim's technical work at the station was also at a standstill.

One day the home phone rang. It was Earl, our Washington attorney.

"Good news. The FCC has approved your application and is issuing you a construction permit today. You're free to go ahead. When you're ready and have completed the necessary program tests submit your data through us for filing. Hopefully they will then act on issuing your license in reasonable time."

"Thanks, Earl, for everything. We'll move quickly," I assured him.

I let out a whoop and gave Tacy the news. I rushed to the station site to share the good news with Jim.

"It's your baby now, Jim. You can call the tower construction company and tell them to go ahead with the tower erection and the ground system installation. We need to get ready to hit the air with program tests. You'll have to post Gordon, who will need to oversee, do the actual signal tests, and check out the transmitter and all the equipment."

"Will do. I'm in good shape. Looks like we can hit the air in a couple of months if the FCC doesn't drag its heels," Jim replied.

"I'll proceed with the staff plans we agreed on for announcers, sales, and office help with a tentative start date — at the outside — July, I hope. We'll arrange some interviews."

Weeks later the tests were completed and the results sent to Washington. The agonizing wait was on again. Furniture and office equipment arrived. Programming sources were finalized, including United Press news teletype service. A record library was completed. Employment interviews were concluded. Finally, the wanted word from Washington came that our license had been granted. We were free to take the air. We were in business officially, but just beginning. I was excited.

f o u r

Radio Rapture

*Man owes his growth, his energy, chiefly to that
striving of the will that conflicts with difficulty,
which we call effort.*

WILLIAM ELLERY CHANNING

On July 10, 1949, at 2 P.M., radio station WTWN,
St. Johnsbury, took to the airwaves, serving an area of
northeastern Vermont and adjacent New Hampshire. The
initial broadcast came live from St. Johnsbury Academy's
Fuller Hall.

The auditorium was packed. The Ambassadors provided
a big band sound on stage, beginning with the *Star Spangled
Banner.* Clergy provided the invocation. Guy, a young, articulate announcer, was master of ceremonies. He introduced
local and state dignitaries including U.S. Senator Ralph
Flanders and Vermont's lone congressman, Charles A.
Plumley, who both offered congratulatory remarks. Letters
from others were read. Staff members were introduced. Jim
and I spoke briefly, offering our sincere gratitude to everyone for their warm welcome and promising our best effort
on their behalf. It was an encouraging on-air start.

WTWN became the only full-time independent radio
station in New England that day. While there was no

national network connection, the station's programming was not just popular records, local news, and news wire service. We soon carried more transcribed radio programs, such as the *Smiths of Hollywood*, produced by Ziv, the nation's largest manufacturer of quality recorded programs, than any station in New England.

Boston Red Sox fans soon heard Curt Gowdy describe a double play at Fenway Park or a home run clout in Yankee Stadium. Football fans could hear mighty Dartmouth stave off an opponent's last-minute threat in the shadow of the goal posts at Memorial Stadium in Hanover, New Hampshire. Local high school and University of Vermont basketball games were also broadcast.

The station carried generous, quality farm programming with the addition of "Uncle Jim" to the staff from WTIC, Hartford, Connecticut. Balanced religious time was offered at no charge. *Midge and That Guy* became a popular morning program and featured everything under the sun. In time, Jerry, an announcer-engineer, became a popular personality as "Mesquite Jerry" on his afternoon *Western Jamboree*. Public service programs abounded and were key. We were community minded, and the young, talented staff applied the Vermont work ethic as a team.

The checkbook balance was skimpy, yes, scary at the start, but the charged-up young staff helped to build funds quickly. One sixty-seven-year-old salesman, Jack, a Lord Calvert type, did his part, too. I knew we couldn't lose with the talented staff we had. The local newspaper had a "new kid on the block," a hungry and ready competitor.

Tacy and I made a lucky move almost across the street to a comfortable townhouse apartment that offered more room and a basement garage. She noticed that I was home only to sleep during the week because of the critical long hours. Weekends brought some relief, with a drive to the mountains, eating out, necessary shopping, and church on Sunday. It was a tough period and demanded mutual understanding. New friends soon added to our limited social life.

By 1951 the station was well established and growing. We began planning to add a similar second station in Newport, a small city some forty miles north on the Canadian border. It sat on the scenic shores of majestic Lake Memphremagog. We formed a second corporation and followed the same procedure as we had with WTWN. We requested the call letters WIKE for the prospective station in honor of General Dwight D. Eisenhower, the famous World War II commander of Allied forces in Europe.

Sales became the focus of my work. I traveled extensively in Vermont and New Hampshire seeking advertisers. We contracted with a national advertising representative firm in New York, which had offices nationwide, and with a regional firm in Boston. There were periodic sales meetings in New York and Boston.

In June 1952, a little blond, blue-eyed daughter, Melissa Lee, smiled her way into our world. She brightened every day. Tacy left her job and centered her work at home. We were happy. I was aware of my new responsibilities and the need to be successful in my radio endeavors.

"Well, if we have another we'll need more room for sure. Need it anyway," I told my wife. She heartily agreed.

On October 12, 1952, Radio Station WIKE took to the air and was connected to WTWN by leased telephone wire. It became the second independent radio station in New England. Collectively they were the North Country Stations of Vermont covering northern portions of two states and adjacent communities in the Province of Quebec.

One day the phone rang in my office, and I took a call from an owner of a new television station in a large Midwestern city.

Dwight D. Eisenhower with the WIKE mike.

"I understand you requested that the call letters WIKE be assigned to your small radio station and that they were. I'm a friend of the general. I'm calling to ask if you would consider changing them so that they could be reassigned to our television station. Naturally we would provide you with reasonable remuneration for the switch."

"I don't think so, sir. I'm sorry," I said.

"Would five thousand dollars change your mind?"

"No, not even if you doubled it. It's no go. The call letters are not for sale," I quickly replied.

He pressed further, and I abruptly ended the call. The general was the Republican candidate for president, and in November he was elected. The timing was perfect. It was a coup and a good omen for a dedicated, young staff.

It wasn't all work in 1952. Life was spiced up by attending a national radio and television broadcasters meeting in Chicago with two staff members. We worked in some entertainment and saw Robert Preston in *The Music Man*, and yelled at a Chicago Black Hawks hockey game that was interrupted by a storm of litter thrown on the ice. I made time for a reunion with an old army buddy too.

A possible future homesite came with a lucky, unexpected purchase of a three-acre lot on a side hill, silhouetted by a grove of towering Norway spruce. It was an overlooked, unusual location, readily adaptable, and just three blocks from Main Street. We had no immediate plans for its use.

During the first half of the fifties life was like an exciting roller coaster ride with a growing family and growing radio stations. In 1953 we took a family trip to North Carolina, where my wife's parents had relocated, giving them an opportunity to be with their first grandchild. It was a good family reunion.

It was payback time. A few days later my mother and I left on a cross-country train ride to Los Angeles. We made some tourist stops before I attended a broadcasters convention. We spent a day in New Orleans, toured the French Quarter, ate in quaint settings, and witnessed a noisy funeral parade.

The next day was a long ride through flatlands and bayous, over some drab expanses of Texas, and to the rim of the

Grand Canyon in the mountains of Arizona for an overnight stay. We were both enthralled by the greatest site either of us had ever seen. I am sure this landscape touched
my mother's spiritual being.

At dinner that night in a fine rustic restaurant on the
rim we had a long, but rarely revealing conversation. We
didn't dwell on the past. Mom never did. She was obviously
thrilled by her present circumstance and I was too. Only
once did the conversation turn to the past — on my part.

"You know, Mom, I really can't remember a lot about
Dad except on trips, swimming, raking leaves, or shoveling
snow, and the hut he put behind the garage for us. I know
he really did a lot for us, and was a fine man and father. I
remember him most for the best thing he ever did for himself, and for us boys."

"What was that?" she asked.

"He married my mother," I said.

We arrived in Los Angeles and checked in at the convention hotel. Between functions we walked Hollywood,
went to the Paladium, went to Will Rogers's ranch, and
viewed the ocean expanse from Santa Monica. That night
we looked down on the shining city and up at the star-loaded
heavens from the observatory.

The trip was valuable, offering me an opportunity to
spend time with my mother and to get to know her even
better. I'd never seen her so relaxed, her face so lit up. My
love and respect for her soared. She was a remarkable woman
— and mother.

The trip ended on a light and funny note. We were tick-
eted to Salisbury, about ten miles from small Coolemee, our
destination. The train whistled, slowed, and came to a grind-
ing halt. It was near dusk. All you could see from the windows were endless fields. There was no sign of a town. The
amiable conductor appeared.

"This is your stop, sir. We can leave you off here in Coolemee to make it more convenient for you folks," he said.

We were elated and thanked him. We took our bags, got off, and set them on the rickety wooden platform adjacent to a dingy shack. Our thanks turned quickly to "no thanks." The station was empty — looked like a remnant of the Civil War. A small weathered sign dangled — COOLEMEE. Soon an elderly farmer arrived in a wagon drawn by two tired horses.

"What you doing here? This ain't no train station anymore," he said.

Needless to say we were now aware of that, but the train wasn't, as I explained to our amused rescuer.

"Well, why don't you folks just climb aboard. I'm headed into town, and I'll take you right to your door."

Gratefully, we did just that, and half an hour later we were greeted by a surprised and laughing family. Our genial friend wouldn't accept a tendered fare — "was comin' into town anyway."

The long trip back to Vermont was marred by a small accident. I inadvertently closed a car door on Melissa's little fingers after coming out of a restaurant. Ice was applied quickly and there was no ongoing problem other than some tears and my wife's anxious comments.

The midfifties were a whirlwind of family and business activity. In 1954, with my mother's help, I purchased a summer cottage on Joe's Pond, an attractive lake in West Danville a few miles from home. Its shoreline was dotted with cottages and second homes for locals and out-of-staters. At one end a small public beach attracted area residents.

The mountain views and colorful sunsets were picture perfect. I remembered the binding family role Buckfield had played in my youth. Perhaps the cottage brought back similar memories to my mother, too. She was a happy, steady summer visitor. The lake cottage was a quiet, welcome family retreat that slowed the pace of life and bonded family. A dream came true for me one day when I returned from a trip to Maine with that handmade green, Old Town wood-and-canvas canoe I had set my heart on years before.

I seriously considered an opportunity to purchase a full-time radio station in Glens Falls, New York. I made an offer, but was rejected. Planning then centered on Springfield, Vermont, one hundred miles south of St. Johnsbury, where we hoped to build a third station in the state.

Springfield once held the lofty position as home to ten percent of the machine tool industry in the United States, but the community was now in decline. The Hartness House, the handsome home of a former governor and now an attractive inn, became the hub for our arrangements to apply for an AM station. This time it had to be for daytime operation only, sunrise to sunset. The manager of the inn, which was owned by local major plants at the time, was Kingsley. He and four leading local businessmen became small stockholders and directors of Connecticut Valley Broadcasting Co.

We bought high-altitude acreage for a tower and transmitter building site. Then we remodeled a store in town to provide offices, a control room, and studio space. The team of Guy and Ken came from WTWN as manager and program director, respectively, for WNIX, named after Vice President Richard Nixon. Young Guy was a dropout student — he had never graduated from high school. He was amazingly self-educated, had a God-given voice, flawless speech, and engineering skills. Ken possessed similar talents and was full of ideas. We were upbeat.

The North Country Stations of Vermont were now three with a staff of thirty-seven energetic young employees and one senior. We worked hard. My adrenaline ran amok, as I did — all over.

In May 1955 the stork delivered Cynthia Deanne to our town house home at Burrows Place. She seemed destined to be a pretty brunette like her mother, maybe a little less rambunctious than her adoring sister. We were admiring and attentive parents. Tacy was a dedicated close-to-home mother and housekeeper in limited space. Cindy was an added joy to our growing family.

Three radio stations and family kept me busy. A fourth opportunity in radio presented itself and I bought a construction permit for a radio station in Barre, the Granite Capital of the World, from a New Hampshire firm. No immediate action was initiated, but preliminary plans were drawn for WSNO, another full-time AM station in a city without one. Life was busy and exciting in the field of radio.

General Eisenhower was now President Eisenhower. He subsequently made a swing through Vermont and New Hampshire with an initial stop at the Rutland Fair in September. We were intent on getting a picture of him holding a WIKE microphone. After a run of failed attempts it happened early one morning "on the green" in Lancaster, New Hampshire. Don thrust the mike to him as he exited his limousine. This time the Secret Service did not interfere. A United Press photographer took a stunning picture of Ike, which he later autographed, and it is now among my most prized possessions.

The Secret Service had interfered on another green the day before when Don, from a distance, was describing Ike's golf game stroke by stroke on our stations. He was doing fine. We were quickly ejected.

I recall an off-year election-night interview with former president Harry Truman, after I had gained his unpublished home telephone number. The mayor of Independence, partying at the country club, had provided Truman's number much to my surprise. After fifty minutes of prior person-to-person calls, the former president answered my station-to-station call.

"Mr. President, Vermont has just elected William Meyer, the first Democrat ever to be elected to our lone seat in the House of Representatives. Would you have any comment, sir?" I asked.

"That's wonderful — that's wonderful," he replied. "It's good for the state. Democrats make better candidates anyway," he added with a hearty laugh. That would be debatable in Vermont. He went on to extend his congratulations to Vermont for becoming a two-party state.

A full recording of the complete interview with the genial former president is among my treasured possessions. His autographed picture arrived soon after the on-air interview. I thought about my vote for Dewey in his upset re-election. I knew I had goofed.

My Vermont broadcasting career was providing me with some light moments near and far. Boston Red Sox games in Fenway Park were a diversion on sales trips to Boston. Trips for meetings in New York afforded the opportunity to see a Yankee game or tennis greats. Chicago evening escapes included conversing with a young, animated Johnny Carson at a hotel bar. The same night four of us laughed until the tears poured forth watching and listening to the antics of Red Skelton.

We took numerous family weekend trips throughout Vermont and the White Mountains of New Hampshire. Vacation trips took us to visit relatives in Connecticut and to the Maine coast. A North Carolina trip to visit grandparents for Christmas was extended to Daytona Beach, Florida, and attractions such as Sea World. The station wagon was always loaded to capacity. The girls were good travelers.

In the summer months the family moved to Joe's Pond,

a dozen miles from the town house. The girls became good swimmers, loved the boat rides, and were thrilled when they caught a fish. We enjoyed many cookouts and evening walks. The girls' growing love for the outdoors was apparent, and mine surged even more.

I did wonder if my wife truly enjoyed camp life. She was not a swimmer. She was a hesitant boat passenger. She didn't have a driver's license and was dependent on me to go anywhere. She did enjoy the cottage and porch. She kept them immaculate and entertained visitors. Several frenzied run-ins with fluttering bats in a bedroom raised her voice and concern. However, Joe's Pond was a treasured family retreat. Mother was a regular two-week summer visitor, and other family members came when they could.

In the late fifties Tacy and I discussed the need to obtain more room for our growing family. We had the land. A sad circumstance advanced our planning when my grandfather died. He who had helped me with a gift to build the first radio station now helped us to build a home. Similar funds passed to my brothers. We contacted a good friend, a local architect, and presented him with our preliminary joint thoughts on building a new colonial home, sinking our roots permanently on that small plateau overlooking Cliff Street. Towering pines and shade trees provided a commanding background. We stressed our own prerequisites and ideas, and he went to work. I turned to other concerns.

Radio in Vermont, as elsewhere, was being challenged by the incursion of television. Vermont was the last of the forty-eight states to give birth to a television station in September 1954. Our radio stations increased local news and sports coverage along with popular music to meet the competition. We also turned to network radio sources for national news and features, first Mutual, then NBC. The advent of FM, frequency modulation radio, was on the horizon offering wider coverage and increased fidelity by its line-of-sight transmission from higher-altitude points. It was just a matter of time before new competition would join the mix.

I tried to determine the right course to follow. In 1957 we abandoned plans for a fourth AM radio station in Barre. The construction permit for WSNO was sold. WNIX in Springfield had made progress in three years, but I made the decision to sell for both business and personal reasons. Daytime AM operation only was a business drawback. The travel distance was an increasing personal problem. Other decisions prompted successful applications for increased power for our two Northeast Kingdom full-time stations, and putting full energies into them. We began to research available FM frequencies.

I met with Carlo Zezza on a hot, sunny day on a roof garden of the Waldorf Astoria in New York City. We talked about selling WNIX in Springfield. I was immediately taken by this articulate, suave figure who sold time for WPIX-TV. He swung a cane, wore a vest, and black spats adorned his shiny shoes. He was an Italian count who, worried about the rise of Mussolini, had immigrated from Italy prior to World War II.

I was ready to sell the Springfield radio station. Carlo was interested in buying. The conversation was lengthy and cordial. We talked about broadcast sales and our experiences.

"I sold the first million-dollar contract for an independent TV station here at WPIX-TV, Channel 11. I like to sell and I can sell TV in New York, or radio in Vermont," he said.

I sensed he could, but I did wonder how this personable city slicker would fare on the limited streets of Springfield, Vermont. In light of his statement and his city demeanor I thought about raising the reasonable price, but didn't. I liked him. We came to an agreement to be refined by attorneys.

"One thing — no station of mine is going to have the call letters WNIX, named for our vice president," he exclaimed. "I want them to be WCFR — *C* for Carlo, *F* for Frank, and *R* for Ruthie — my son and daughter."

"It will be your station and that's your baby if they aren't already assigned to another station — probably aren't," I said.

The transfer was processed in reasonable time, and Carlo and his family moved to a small town in Vermont. I was pleasantly surprised by his adjustment to country living. Carlo came to love Vermont. The family bought a small farm not far from town and were joined by a host of barnyard animals — a big change from the sidewalks of Manhattan. Vermont does get to you.

I now turned my efforts exclusively to the Northeast Kingdom, to the original two radio stations, and to family considerations. Ken, who had built our radio stations, started on a split-level, white-clapboard, colonial home with three distinct living sections on the first floor: a combination kitchen, family room, and dining area; a large, central, formal living room; and a three-bedroom wing with two baths. There was a half-bath and laundry area off the kitchen. Old bricks were used in the family-room fireplace, new for the one in the living room.

A basement area under one wing contained the heating plant, a sizable recreation room with a fieldstone fireplace and plain, weathered boards on the walls. There was also a half-bath. The rest was accessible crawl space. There was an outside entrance.

Simple planning led to cherished comfort and quality work at a surprisingly reasonable cost. After all, we weren't building in Greenwich. Tacy handled the interior decorating. A large two-car garage with overhead storage was added. Cement-slate walkways and steps followed.

Our home was within easy walking distance to church,

schools, and the business district. It was a real help to Tacy, and the girls could walk to school until they went off to college. We enjoyed the friendly neighborhood and we all took great pride in our new home. It was a hectic, exciting time.

The setting was picturesque: seventeen Norway spruce towering one hundred and fifty feet dominated the home's wooded backdrop. Vermont's legendary fall foliage splattered color onto the scene. Winter snows on sagging limbs created a fairyland. They also brought heavy shoveling of walks and driveway. Sometimes it took extra runs to get the car into the garage, but we loved our new home, and its rich, nature-touched surroundings.

I enjoyed planting a hedge, shrubbery, a few small trees on the lawn, and working on the lawn and flower beds. In time we added a productive vegetable garden. The girls helped. My wife concentrated her efforts inside the home. Life took a new tack.

five

Turbulent Times

It is the content of our lives that determines their value. If we limit ourselves to supply the means of living, in what way have we placed ourselves above the cattle that graze the land?

A. H. COMPTON

My radio career was blessed from the outset by the young men and women who joined me in the effort. In the sixties I turned to increasing my outside interests, all but one in the public service. I put up with being a bank director for a limited time, but it wasn't my cup of tea.

My service as the first president of the Vermont Association of Broadcasters was stimulating. My service as a trustee of a local hospital, as its treasurer, and then as its president was likewise. I will always wonder about one touching, emotional experience when a young new hospital administrator called with a disturbing message.

"We have a young girl here and I'm told by the doctors that she needs immediate surgery to save her life. Her parents have refused to consent because of their religious beliefs. The girl's life hangs in the balance. What do we do?" he asked.

"I'll call our attorney to ask about the legal ramifications

. . . will arrange to meet there right away," I replied.

We convened in the small office and were joined by a surgeon who described the girl's life-threatening situation. I found it difficult to understand the parents' steadfast religious position, as did the others. After some phone calls we found a major medical center that would accept her as a transfer patient. A doctor there was willing to try an alternative method to save her life. The sound of the ambulance taking off brought sighs of relief. I still wonder about the outcome but have the strong feeling that she came through her ordeal.

My wife and I were both active in our church and I found increasing spiritual credence while being a deacon for three years. The girls attended Sunday school and a private kindergarten before entering the public school system.

In 1963 I served on the local school board — the only new member to be elected — and went on to serve six additional years as chairman. It was the start of an almost second career that proved interesting, controversial, and challenging. The year was an important milestone for me and my adopted state.

Philip Hoff, thirty-six, a lawyer and first-term legislator, became the first Democrat governor elected by the people since 1828. It was an historic event. The *Burlington Free Press* called his inaugural address "one of the boldest in the State's history." The *Bennington Banner* printed "one of the first refreshing breezes to blow into state government in a long time." I was impressed and cast my first vote for a Democrat seeking public office.

In midyear I obtained a radio interview with Richard Griebel, president of Fairbanks, Morse & Company. Their old plant in St. Johnsbury constituted the area's largest employer. The interview also served as a reminder of the historic and benevolent past of the Fairbanks family. He indicated the company was objectively evaluating the future of their hundred-year-old facility. Relocation was a possibility. A copy of the taped interview was aired, dispatched to the governor, and provided a warning to Vermont and the affected areas.

A major drive was soon launched to keep Fairbanks, Morse & Company in St. Johnsbury. In an expression of Vermont energy, ingenuity, and common purpose, local area citizens raised over $500,000 in a matter of days for the Fairbanks Foundation. The Fairbanks family had long endowed the community with valuable assets and everyone knew it. The overall financial package led the company to stay and build a 340,000-square-foot plant and offices on a new fifty-acre site.

The spirit was contagious. When the going gets tough Vermonters get tougher. It was a major example of neighbor helping neighbor — as it should be. Keeping the plant in the area was an economic necessity, but it was also payback for the generous outpourings of the Fairbanks family in prior years.

My work on the local school board was stimulating and rewarding. Considerations were minor, major, and sometimes heated. They included curriculum and teachers, leaky school roofs, budget problems, and closing small outmoded buildings. In the midsixties the state designated St. Johnsbury as an Area Vocational Center site. The new Vermont policy stipulated that vocational education must be developed in comprehensive high schools rather than through specialized vocational schools such as the St. Johnsbury Trade School.

This led to long, complicated, and controversial negotiations with the trustees of St. Johnsbury Academy, a distinctive, elitist-run private school serving as the local area's public high school. The goal — to arrange a marriage between the public Johnsbury Trade School and the respected private academy.

It was a normal day in the radio station and staff members were engaged in routine work. Conversations were marked by an occasional laugh, and low, on-air music filtered through the area. Shortly after noon the clanging United Press teletype machine signaled a news bulletin. President Kennedy had been shot in Dallas. The bulletin was finalized quickly with the statement: "The President was declared dead at 1 P.M. at Parkland Hospital, Dallas."

The staff was in total shock. Tears rolled down cheeks in an outpouring of overwhelming grief. Conversations subsided and people stood in disbelieving silence. It was a scene I will never forget. I thought of the young and captivating U.S. senator I had once met in Burlington who had earned my respect and admiration as president. I idolized him.

Our stations ceased commercial advertising, retreated to appropriate classical and religious music, and arranged for complete network news and funeral coverage. It was a sad and sobering time. I never saw grief displayed so deeply, so automatically, so collectively.

Radio stations and educational matters continued to dominate my work world. The family was happy in our new home and enjoying summer days at Joe's Pond. The girls were growing, healthy, and busy.

The school board proceeded with building plans and determining costs for an area vocational center, hiring an out-of-state architectural firm. It took many months to complete plans, determine costs, and reach a final consensus. It was a demanding time with many additional meetings and delicate negotiations for the school board and superintendent. In the meantime, the governor appointed me to a nine-member temporary advisory commission on the reorganization of school districts in the state.

In 1966 the governor called and asked me to run for a state senate seat from my county. The incumbents were two Republicans. One was Doug, a close friend — moderate, competent, and forward-looking. The other was George, "Dean of the Senate," with twenty-one years of service. I must admit I thought he was too old and out of touch (at about the same age I am writing this). I do recall saying, "He doesn't pay a minimum wage on his farm." He was a soft-spoken, respected, and conservative Republican.

"Governor, I'm not a Democrat," I said. "I'm really an Independent, but I come from a staunch Republican family and background. . . . I want to help you, but I don't think it fits."

"Okay, I understand where you're coming from . . . so run as an Independent."

I was flattered by his call, and thought highly of him as a person and governor. I finally agreed to take the plunge as an Independent. Maybe he was just trying to boost his message and voter turnout in our county in his reelection bid for a third term. Some felt that he had lost support in the area.

My decision to run soon after received the endorsement and support of the Democratic Party. I didn't seek contributions and spent only a few hundred dollars of my own. I took off and learned a lot about Vermonters trekking door-to-door throughout the county. It was an educational effort that molded, broadened, and hardened my opinions as nothing ever had. I met all kinds of people, saw how they lived, and heard all kinds of things. The experience increased my respect for Vermonters and their way of life. With one or two exceptions I was treated courteously.

The governor carried the county handsomely, and was returned to office. I lost in the spirited three-way race with a credible showing, carrying my hometown with Doug. I honestly didn't expect to win. The experience was a good education and demonstrated my concern for the continuing need for a strong two-party system in Vermont. The election loss actually turned out to be a win in a sense, leading to an opportunity more in line with my experience and interests. The governor appointed me to a six-year term on the Vermont State Board of Education in March 1967. For a time this work overlapped with my duties as chairman of the local school board. It was a demanding, but interesting time.

As a member of the State Board of Education I became enmeshed at the state level in struggles to establish the vocational center in my own area. Recognizing that all students are not college bound, I found myself favoring the regionalization of many schools except when extenuating circumstances made it unacceptable. I also accepted an invitation to become a trustee for a small, innovative private academy being established in the county. The chairman of the State Board of Education did likewise. Our basic input was to provide help and coordination at the state level.

A war of words was waged in the state over the *Vermont Design for Education,* written by the outspoken education commissioner, Dr. Harvey Scribner, which I strongly supported. The text emphasized "the freedom to learn, responsibility not permissiveness, learning to live with people, and helping to right a society ripped by hatred, prejudice and suspicion." It is still relevant.

The *Vermont Design* stressed flexibility in approach and called for local initiative, responsibility, and assessment. The accent was right where most Vermonters like it. Opponents countered with expressions such as, "It will not prepare young people for the monotony and routine of the business world." They obviously had blinders on and suffered from pessimism. I believed it would help young people to step into an exciting and challenging world of opportunity.

I remember taking issue with a $165,000 state study on reorganization that was politically motivated and narrow in scope. I invoked the words of Robert Finch, "American classrooms need a shaking-up to improve teaching. Many of our elementary schools are now teaching the way they did twenty years ago." It was true in Vermont. One small school spent $3.25 in 1967–68 for library books, periodicals, and audio-visual learning aids.

In January 1968 the voters of St. Johnsbury flocked to the polls to decide the fate of the proposed Area Vocational Center. By just a two vote margin, citizens turned down a proposal for construction in the amount of $2,462,300. By a similar margin voters approved the 1.1 million dollar bond for the project. Voter turnout on the local issue was the highest in the previous twenty years. The result was muddled and disappointing. The state granted an extension for a second try, allowing more time for study and for educating the public.

In April a critical stumbling block to the project was finally eliminated when the academy's board of trustees voted to "accept responsibility for the administration and operation of the proposed St. Johnsbury Area Vocational Center."

A second vote soon followed and went down to defeat by a slightly larger margin. It was all a compelling challenge, a frustrating undertaking, but rewarding in the end. A third attempt was again quickly mounted and this time it was approved by a razor-thin margin.

Construction and the funds for it were authorized. The end result was construction of a 72,000-square-foot building adjacent to the academy campus. It was built at a projected cost of $2,462,000. It did not come easily, and it didn't set well with many. It did underscore the old adage that "if you don't succeed, try, try again." I felt it was a worthy accomplishment in the best interests of our young people and those to follow. I felt good.

My seven years on the school board and my controversial stands led to a narrow three vote defeat at the town caucus for renomination as a candidate for the school board. I chose not to contest the verdict with an independent candidacy. It was over on the local scene. I was already in the larger state educational arena and involved in the partisan politics associated with it. My earlier naive thoughts that politics don't belong in education were long gone. I left many meetings disturbed by this. I was admittedly uptight on occasion, chairing a meeting as vice chairman under the glare of television and other media coverage.

Early one evening I headed home after a particularly grueling meeting. I was tired and didn't feel well. It was all I could do to make it home. The feeling was similar to something that had hit me driving on the Jersey Turnpike in an earlier year when the family was returning from North Carolina. This time the doctor prescribed a tranquilizer and some needed rest.

On the home front my daughters were involved in Girl Scouts and my wife got involved in overseeing cookie sales. Both girls attended national camporees in the West at different times. Both were good students and active in school and church activities. Both skied and played tennis. Cindy was a hot softball catcher. They weren't great kitchen and housekeeping helpers — a role my wife excelled in — but they didn't mind getting their hands dirty in the garden or using a snow shovel.

My daughters and I conspired to make one Memorial Day doubly noteworthy. We went to nearby New Hampshire and returned with a five-week-old, buff, male cocker spaniel we had arranged to buy. It didn't set well with my wife, who was skittish about dogs, and she made her feelings plainly known.

Corky enriched our home and also the cottage at Joe's

Pond. He lived for fourteen years and was a lovable companion, even for Tacy — a member of the family. For me it was a return to earlier dog-devoted days.

I found some recreational diversion in downhill skiing but my companions' abilities were far beyond mine. They would make three runs to my slow, twist-and-turn descents. I couldn't afford a broken leg, was cautious, and mindful of a previous hairline kneecap fracture — not from skiing. I had been on a ladder painting garage shingles one afternoon when I encountered an angry swarm of hornets. I bolted, fell on a cement walk, and had lingering pain. The next day I had a rigid walking cast on my right leg — just hell for driving. I crossed my left foot to the gas pedal and brake.

I had some overriding interests and concerns — the future of the radio stations, education in which I was increasingly involved, and family. I was constantly on the go during the day and many evenings. My wife stuck close to home, just like her mother in many respects. Weekends normally provided family time and eating out. However, the routine Saturday afternoon supermarket and shopping trip used to get to me. July and August at Joe's Pond provided some welcome relief, relaxing activities, and family fun.

The turn into the seventies provided no respite from controversial education decisions at the state level. I took some parting shots at proponents of a bill to change the status of the state board that reflected a partisan, political effort aimed at having the education commissioner appointed by the governor, reducing the State Board of Education to a purely advisory role.

I testified before the Committee on Government Operations in the House of Representatives stating that education is the very guts of society, the very soul of everything dear to us. Education is not a partisan matter any more than motherhood. Vermont youth are better served if education is insulated as much as possible from political influence and left in the hands of a lay policy-making board and a commissioner not responsible to a politically appointed undersecretary, or the governor. Others testified both for and against such legislation. It did not become law.

Melissa was nearing high school graduation and college. The family visited a number of colleges after she gleaned information that aroused interest. Most were outside New England — in New York, Pennsylvania, and then Virginia, which led to a decision.

Melissa and I sought advice from a friend of mine, the director of admissions at my alma mater, Washington and Lee University in Virginia, an all-male college. He strongly recommended Roanoke College in Salem, an hour away. "It's coed, academically high, and just a great place."

The next morning we arrived on the attractive campus and parked in front of the admissions office.

"Dad, I don't want to go here. I'm not doing the interview," my daughter said.

She had an appointment and her application was filled out. With some urging she went in. A little later she came out smiling, expressed real interest, and we toured the campus. She was impressed by everyone she met and everything she saw. Her sister took it all in too and was favorably impressed as well. It ended college touring. Melissa was accepted for entry in September 1970. We were pleased with her choice. A few years later Cindy joined her on campus for her freshman year. They both loved their college days. We bought another car for them to use at college, easing transportation to and from home.

One quiet evening at home the phone rang and it was Melissa. The usual happy tone was missing. Her words came slowly, carefully chosen. "Dad, the car is gone," she said.

"What do you mean? Has there been an accident?"

She gave me the surprising details.

"Dad, late afternoon yesterday I was going to a mall in Roanoke, and I stopped at a traffic light at a major intersection. A guy on the side of the road popped out. He had a gun and he told me to move over so he could drive. He made a turn, and we drove off into a mountainous area. I was scared and I pleaded with him. He was a young white guy. . . .

"It was getting dark. He finally stopped on a dead-end road in a heavily wooded area. Well, you know the Vega seat belts that come across when you shut the car door. I released the seat belt, sprung the door, ran into the woods as far as I could, fell flat, and didn't dare move. He got out with the high beams on but he didn't try to come after me. I think I surprised him. A couple of minutes later he floored the gas pedal and sped off."

"Thank God for that. Are you okay? Where are you? What about the Vega?" I said.

"Dad, I was afraid to come out and go down the road again. I thought he might be there. I kept going into the woods deeper and deeper, and I finally came to a river. I followed it and came to a farm. The people were home and were real nice to me. I explained what happened, and then I called the state police and told them everything."

"You used your head, honey. We're real proud — but go on."

"Dad, they found the Vega — what was left of it — not far from where he kidnapped me. He torched it with gasoline, so they couldn't get his fingerprints maybe. They were able to identify a college sticker on the bumper so the police had already called the college. They contacted Cindy who told them where I had gone, but said that I wasn't back. A state trooper came to get me at the farm, and now I'm back in the dorm. I'm okay, Dad. They want me to go down to police headquarters, look at some mug shots."

"Right now I'm sure you need some rest. It's been a harrowing experience, but thank God you kept your head. . . . We love you," I said.

She finally burst into tears, and said to me, "But, Dad, the car you got for us is gone. I'm sorry. It cost a lot of money."

"The car is minor. We have insurance. It will be replaced as soon as I can arrange it and I'll drive it down as soon as possible. The heck with the car. You're okay, and that's all we care about. You kept your cool and we are just so proud of you. I can imagine how Cindy reacted to all this too. . . . Talk to you soon. Love to you both."

A five-state alarm for the abductor was fruitless. The college, possibly taking a cue from my daughter's ordeal, greatly improved lighting on the campus after the event.

The burned Vega, covered by insurance, was immediately replaced by our reliable and concerned dealer. I drove it to Virginia and a friend followed in my car for the return trip. There was a surprise. We pulled off for a rest stop at the New Market Battlefield Museum on I-81. We returned to find the left front fender and hood collapsed on the tire. The car was going nowhere.

I muttered something about General Motors in disbelief, but thanked my lucky stars it hadn't happened at high speed on the highway. The new car was hauled off to a local dealership, and a week later my daughter picked up a General Motors replacement in Harrisonburg. She came through her kidnapping ordeal in amazingly good shape, but I suspected it would always be a reminder that life does have unexpected moments over which you have no control.

At home, my six years on the Vermont State Board of Education came to a close. With daughters in college and changing interests, we sold the family camp at Joe's Pond. The St. Johnsbury Area Vocational Center was dedicated, and young people who weren't college bound had their future horizons lifted. It was well worth the long struggle and I was gratified by the reward.

However, I grew increasingly unsettled with my personal life but hid it as best I could. I really wasn't happy. Strangely, I was both active and bored. I agonized over my marriage, particularly conscious of my two daughters. I wanted fulfillment. I wanted more than I had, but that didn't mean dollars or material possessions. I thought about values and new convictions. I reflected on mistakes.

One night I substituted for the highly respected moderator at our church meeting. There was heated debate on a motion to establish a coffee house in available space within the building for our young people to meet and talk among themselves and with those of other denominations. The room would have separate outside access. I saw it as a step to meet a vital need in the community and the Christian thing to do. I asked permission to speak and did — in favor. The motion was overwhelmingly defeated.

I believe we failed our young people and conveyed the wrong impression. Perhaps I overreacted, but I made the decision to leave the church along with three other members including a dedicated high school teacher. The girls were in college. My wife raised no objection. I found a welcome at St. Andrew's Episcopal Church a few doors away.

I vented some of my frustrations by editorializing on the radio but generally avoided the field of education. One editorial on handgun control is illustrative. I said handguns and Saturday night specials are responsible for 54 percent of all murders in the country, yet they account for less than 20 percent of the total firearms in civilian hands. I explained that the National Rifle Association, with a membership of over a million and a budget of ten million dollars, was lobbying successfully to block any type of federal legislation that would require stricter accountability on handguns and handgun owners. Times haven't changed — only the figures.

It was a hectic period with the unpopular Vietnam War in the background, with civil strife on urban streets, and unrest on college campuses. It was in this milieu that I accepted a six-year appointment to the Vermont State Colleges Board. I saw it as a natural extension of my experience in the field of education, as well as an opportunity to learn and to contribute.

Budget cutbacks and cost controls became the name of the game as enrollment at the state colleges plummeted due to the draft and the relatively high tuition costs. The chancellor of the system was heavily under fire, often out front, and taking unpopular necessary positions that I usually supported.

I retain a personal perception of the Vietnam tragedy drawn from Bryan, a young veteran from our hometown "who saw it all." He attended a state college where I taught a course in broadcasting for a semester. I knew his family and got to know him well. He was bright, motivated, and had excellent potential. We had some lengthy discussions, often turning to political topics.

On his graduation I hired him as a newsman at the local radio station and he got off to a good start. In time, tardiness set in and his work slipped. I believed the war was still ravaging him and I stumbled on the possible indication of drug use. He told me he would mend his ways. We talked about a lot of things. I saw real potential in Bryan and tried to help bring it out.

My own life continued at a fast pace. In a way it was routine and my interest waned in some areas. In outward appearances I am sure my marriage seemed fine. Inwardly I felt a gnawing uneasiness — that lack of fulfillment. Tacy and I just weren't on the same wavelength. My heavy involvement in outside activities both compensated for and contributed to the problem.

The relationship was gradually becoming platonic, the spark flickered. We shared few common interests except our children and our lovely home. I thought of separation for a number of years, always putting it off because of concern for my two daughters. I knew what it meant not to have a father. I was conscious of my responsibility.

I had simmering thoughts about finding a radio station in Virginia. When I heard that the station in Lexington might be sold, I contacted the owners and went to Virginia to meet with them. They had another buyer, but there was a legal problem involving an out-of-town stockholder who had reservations about the sale and was holding things up. I was encouraged to submit an offer. I did and it was higher. However, it was too late to undo papers already signed and declared legally binding. I lost out, but didn't give up the idea of looking further in the Shenandoah Valley of Virginia.

I soon returned to Virginia to investigate another radio station in the attractive larger city of Harrisonburg. An initial meeting with the owner offered real encouragement. We talked extensively and it became apparent that he was considering changes at the station that included a possible sale. We hit it off and made arrangements to meet again while I was in the area.

A day later I had Bryan fly to Virginia, believing that there was a strong possibility I could open the door to a sale, or buy in and take over the management. I thought Bryan just might fit into the picture if it could ever jell. We went to dinner with the owner and a close friend and engaged in further promising discussion. We had a good exchange and further communication was assured. I became interested in a personal move there too.

Bryan showed promise in the news area and took particular pride in covering the New Hampshire primary for our stations. He privately interviewed two governors, Carter and Reagan, candidates for president. I wondered if he had unloaded his thoughts about Vietnam on them.

Then tragedy struck. Bryan was found hanged in his apartment on Easter weekend. The community was crushed. The outpouring at his funeral was overwhelming. I struggled to do the eulogy at his service. He was truly a casualty of the war itself just as if he had died in action. He was a remarkable young man and a good friend. He was close to his family and particularly to Jason, a brother twelve years his junior. I felt his loss deeply. He was too young. What a waste. His name is now rightfully inscribed on the Vietnam Memorial as a casualty.

In the midst of all these changes I made regular trips to Virginia's Shenandoah Valley during my daughters' six overlapping college years at Roanoke College. Both enjoyed their years there and pulled good marks. Both joined the same sorority and dated at nearby Washington and Lee, participating in functions at my old fraternity house. Their grandmother often accompanied my wife and me on visits and she attended both of their graduations. They were close.

Melissa elected to pursue a master's degree in social work and gained admission to the University of Kentucky. Her undergraduate record earned her scholarship aid, and in her second year she was rewarded with an assistantship. We made a number of trips to the area, the handsome horse farms always catching our attention.

Cindy graduated from college with a bachelor's degree in social work too. She opted initially to remain in the area, gaining her first job in psychiatric social services associated with a major hospital. She later elected to move back to New England, taking a position with a crisis management organization centering on a variety of difficult one-on-one personal crisis problems at all hours. I admired her ability and work but sensed it was mentally draining and would be short lived.

Melissa returned to Virginia after obtaining her masters in social work, taking a position with the Girl Scouts of America handling a branch office in Staunton. Her work centered on troop development and services in the Shenandoah Valley area. Her office was located in Trinity Episcopal Church, founded as Augusta Parish House in 1746. The original building served as the Revolutionary capitol of Virginia for sixteen days in 1781.

The absence of our daughters from home affected the marriage. Our major tie loosened. Face to face we were non-communicative about the marriage itself. My world was busy outside the home and she did not get involved. Her world was basically in our beautiful home and keeping it that way. A few friends, television, and the telephone enhanced her days. She walked the few blocks "over town," or to church, but otherwise depended on me for transportation. I should have insisted she obtain a driver's license, but there was no inclination on her part. It was a major mistake and severely constrained both our lives.

Silently I reacted negatively to her sedentary existence and accompanying weight problem. I held it in, but it gnawed on me. It was troubling — even sad. Looking back there should have been more attention to her feet and the walking problems that developed over several years. Our relationship lacked the ingredients it needed to flourish. There was no real warmth. She was painstakingly slow and I was the opposite. She was an indoor person. I was not. She was a night owl. I was not. We maintained respect for each other. There were no words — no abuse.

I wondered — what do we now have in common beyond our girls, our families, and our home? We certainly joined in a common and successful effort to raise our daughters and to do our best for them. We enjoyed many wonderful years as a family in that overriding pursuit. The future was a mounting dilemma. The union was not fulfilling and the road ahead uncertain. What to do?

On a May evening in 1976 I entered a small unpretentious country church in Hardwick, Vermont, the Episcopal Mission of St. John the Baptist. The preacher and celebrant was the Right Reverend Robert S. Kerr, bishop of the Episcopal Church in Vermont. Standing in front of him, I was confirmed in the Episcopal Church, experienced the Holy Eucharist, and found a new peace.

It was no reflection on the church and its fine people I had left. I just needed more than I was getting to feed my own spirituality. I believe I found it. I felt new strength to handle some agonizing problems and more confident to face the future.

On the way home my quiet thoughts turned to my mother and her abiding faith in God and prayer. They turned to my own family. They also drifted back to my freshman year in college when I seriously considered a career in the ministry. I had met with other similar students, local ministers, and worked some at a mountain mission in Appalachia. I think Mother ascribed those early feelings to a passing fancy. She was usually right.

My change nourished and sustained me. It brought a new sense of peace and direction into my life. I felt it strongly as I looked forward to communion and kneeling with others at every service. It was a very special time for me. Peter, the young rector, a graduate of Yale Divinity School, was devoted and upbeat — full of love and life. He was a good listener, a good speaker, and a good counselor. He was probably a little ahead of his time for some older parishioners. For me he became a warm and caring friend as well as my minister.

s i x

Personal Upheaval

Sorrow never gets tired of its sadness, as the wind gets tired of blowing: The prosperous are not always prosperous, or else they were not prosperous. Change is the mistress of all things. Therefore, he that hopeth is wise, and he that despaireth is a fool.

EURIPIDES

In the summer of 1976 an unraveling started that led to the best years of my life — and the worst. One day in June a good friend dropped by my office. He asked if we had any openings at the radio stations for his daughter, Barbara. She had just graduated from college majoring in political science and was bent on a journalism career in broadcasting.

I knew his daughter had attended high school with my daughters, and I had high regard for the family. We went to the same church. I told my friend that unfortunately we had no openings in our news operations, but that I would try to supply some leads. I did make a few contacts without success in the days ahead.

My interest in journalism was strong and I felt that news dissemination was critical to gaining listeners and meeting our print competition. I felt a real need to editorialize and did on occasion. Now and then a print editorial in the local paper ticked me off. The public needed another perspective.

We were pleased and proud of our upgrade to CBS radio news for national and world news. We received most state and regional news via United Press teletype service. But we lacked the staff to cover our local and Northeast Kingdom area adequately. It would be helpful to have a person capable of investigative and in-depth reporting. My friend's call renewed my determination to cover local and area news better. However, because of other priorities the intent bubbled on a back burner. Acquiring a Virginia station was still on my mind.

Barbara's search for broadcast news employment bore no immediate fruit. Her father queried me again weeks later. I remembered that the Vermont Association of Broadcasters would be having their annual meeting at the Jay Peak Ski Resort. Bill, our station manager in nearby Newport, was in charge of all arrangements. We needed help on an information and registration desk during the three-day event. I thought of Barbara, who would have the opportunity to make valuable contacts with broadcast executives from all over the state. She was an ideal choice — attractive, intelligent, and responsible. I called and she enthusiastically accepted. Fate was in the offing.

I arrived early on Friday afternoon for a planned tennis match, and found Barbara on duty. I had rarely seen her during her college years. Her pretty brown hair touched her shoulders. Her smile radiated with warmth and accented her dimples. She had matured and I was immeasurably impressed overall.

The following day I opted for more tennis and a swim. I also talked with Barbara about her college years and radio in general. We had often talked at Dunkin' Donuts in her high school years. I continued to be impressed by her. That evening when the day's program ended, Barbara and I sought refuge from the hotel's stifling heat. We went outside to take a walk and breathe the fresh mountain air.

The moon, stars, and mountains combined to make a breathtaking panorama. We walked and small-talked along the peaceful paths. I felt happy and relaxed. Our talk turned to nature and the outdoors, naturally prompted by the inspiring surroundings.

"Mountains are the beginning and the end of all scenery," I said, quoting John Ruskin.

We talked about our families, her college years, my radio years, and our lives in general. It poured out easily.

"I majored in political science," she said. "I'm interested in government, politics, and social issues. I like to read and write, and am interested in journalism, but really in broadcast as opposed to print media. Maybe television someday if I can make it. Who knows?"

I thought to myself — I know. She is smart, personable, and photogenic. That will help. She's a go-getter too.

Now and then we shared a good laugh, and our conversation hit lighter subjects such as skiing, soccer, and swimming. She was obviously athletic. She said she jogged every day and was a vegetarian. I had noted her license plate — VEGGY.

At one point our hands touched and then clasped firmly. We looked at each other. Our walking gait picked up some and so did my heart rate. Soon we came to the deserted tramway base station with its cables and towers climbing into the clouds. I will never forget that first spontaneous embrace. We soon walked back to the hotel and to our separate rooms. If nothing else a warm friendship was astir, but there was no discussion of employment. I concluded her spirit, her maturity, and her potential would surely impress a future employer.

I saw Barb the next morning before I went to a round of

meetings. She was busy and we spoke briefly. There was no reference to the night before. I presumed she would make some contacts with prospective employers throughout the day.

I took a short walk outside to mull things over. I recognized her talent and knew our news coverage needed a good boost. She was local and a natural with her qualifications. She was remarkably mature and informed for her age. I decided to talk to her further — maybe hire her. I spoke to her and arranged to meet her the following week in our hometown.

Back at home, Barbara and I took a talkative ride to the White Mountains ending atop a fire tower in a mountain park. The conversation centered on radio and her job search but touched on other topics too. I described my criticism of our news efforts in detail, and outlined what was needed. She made constructive comments. She was open and direct. We talked and talked. We had a lot in common.

I made up my mind right there that I would not let her go. I turned to her and outlined some employment arrangements.

"You're hired, Barb, if you can accept what I've outlined. I'm sure you can handle it, and I will help you all I can. What do you say?"

She smiled, and said, "Oh, yes."

I certainly didn't realize then where it would lead and how it would affect our lives. She was twenty-three, and I was thirty years her senior. I didn't give it a thought. I am sure she didn't.

Barb moved back to town, joined our staff as news director, and added in-depth and investigative reporting to our efforts. She developed a feature program, *The Northeast Corner*, digging deeply into many subjects including government, the environment, and social issues. A self-starter, she quickly proved her ability and work ethic. I felt my decision was vindicated from a business standpoint. I was quietly reeling with admiration for this determined young woman. Her future was taking shape. Mine too.

Heavy involvement in business, community, and state activities kept me busy and increasingly affected my lackluster marriage. I am not one to accept routine and boredom. Over the weeks and months, with my daughters in college, Barbara became the light of my life. Our values, interests, activities, and feelings found common ground. We balanced our professional conduct and our personal feelings.

We grew close. There seemed to be no generation gap. Her sense of humor helped. We sandwiched our busy schedules with hours together on and off the job. She became another tennis opponent — a good one. Now and then we slipped off to take a hike. On one occasion, accepting her smiling challenge, I raced down a long grassy slope on her heels and tumbled on her at the bottom. Chagrined, I drove myself to the hospital over her objection. I had my broken wrist set, put in a cast, and went home with no one the wiser about all the actual details.

I have a poignant memory of a another minor incident. Barb arrived at my home in a car driven by Sterry, a good friend and United States District Court judge. He was highly respected and an original small stockholder in the local radio station. The revered United States Senator George Aiken, author of the Northeast Kingdom name, was the other passenger. Barb was going to cover a major news event at a nearby college, and they invited her to accompany them. In turn, I was also invited, perhaps in light of my being a member of the state colleges board.

In a sense it proved fortunate. At the conclusion of the event we found the judge's car locked with the keys in the ignition. It was a bitter subzero night and snowing. Much to my surprise and theirs, I opened the car door with the aid of a bent wire coat hanger from a college cloakroom, and off we went.

"That really showed ability. Have you had a lot of experience? I thought you were full time in the radio business. Do you have another nighttime vocation?" the senator jokingly asked.

Barbara's reputation grew and she helped it with her many contacts and her nose for news. She was invited to accompany high-level state officials on a business trip to Switzerland, and the station shared in some reasonable expense incurred. She regularly fed numerous stories to United Press wire service. She used her head and was a professional reporter. Her energy level helped.

I switched from downhill skiing to cross-country where I could set my own pace and curtail the possibility of injury. Barbara was an excellent cross-country skier, and she initiated cross-country skiing instruction at the local country club on Sunday afternoons for a number of weeks. It was a great opportunity for me. I jumped. I needed instruction. My wife confronted me after I went a few times.

"I don't want you going up there on Sunday afternoons for lessons anymore," she said in no uncertain terms.

I didn't pursue the subject. I sensed a problem. Perhaps it was the instructor with whom I also played tennis on occasion. I ceased without comment and shifted to nearby cross-country trails utilizing what I had learned. Barb usually joined me. I loved cross-country skiing in the winter as much as I loved my canoeing in the summer. Nothing was more peaceful and invigorating than gliding through dense forests of snow-covered evergreens or barreling down grades in an open field. It was even more fun with Barbara along as I tried to keep up with her.

In the midseventies my work life was devoted to all aspects of the radio stations, particularly management and sales work, studying and planning for FM, serving on the state colleges board, and being involved in public service activities.

I made a number of trips to larger markets in Virginia and New York State to evaluate stations for sale. I combined a trip to Virginia with a visit to my daughter. One evening I accompanied her to a Girl Scout meeting in Monterey, a rural mountain community. She drove her Volkswagen home over steep, slippery mountain roads in a blowing, blinding snowstorm. My heart was in my throat the whole way. She was her usual calm and steady self. My thoughts again returned to her dangerous ride into the mountains with a kidnapper and his gun.

Barbara's talent and hard work paid off for her and for our radio stations. We received word that she would be recognized by United Press International at an awards dinner in Boston in their New England news competition. Barbara and I were present when her program, *The Northeast Corner,* won a third-place citation for excellence in the highly competitive program category. We were elated and she had real reason to be proud. It was well earned. I knew she had a good future in broadcasting.

There's an old saying from the 1700s attributable to James Boswell: "We cannot tell the precise moment when friendship is formed. As in filling a vessel drop by drop, there is at last a drop which makes it run over; so in a series of kindnesses, there is at last one which makes the heart run over."

That pretty well describes my situation with Barbara. My heart ran over with her kindnesses and much more. She was so natural, so effervescent, so active, and so much fun. Our interests, our thoughts, our feelings had common ground. She made me happy so easily. I respected her and her ways. She was also a private individual, but we could talk about anything. We held nothing back. I knew her. She knew me. She became my best friend — and more.

One afternoon, conscious of our growing relationship, we shared it with her local minister in his study. He was gracious, cautious, but helpful. His remarks personified his genuine caring character. We left somewhat relieved by his words.

In the summer, while my wife and daughter visited friends in Connecticut, I left for a business meeting and tied it in with meeting Barbara. She was returning from a week's vacation to the Rockies with a friend who left her off near Poughkeepsie, New York.

Nostalgia got the best of me and on the way home I took her to see Lake Minnewaska in the mountains close by — hardly comparable to the Rockies, but still captivating to any eye.

We sipped on a cold drink in the aging Wildmere Hotel and then took a hike around the pristine lake with its hovering rocky crags and ledges. The same gray wooden summerhouses dotted the landscape around the lake, shutting out the sun's hot rays. There was hardly a ripple on the smooth inviting surface of the water. The trail took us on pine-strewn paths along the water's edge, over stepping-stones in a shallow cove, and up the timber staircases and rocky pathways to my favorite double-decker summerhouse overlooking the magical scene.

We had the place to ourselves except for a few scurrying squirrels and the delicate butterflies fluttering around the wildflower and wild blueberry patches. We caught our breath, sat, and relaxed in conversation.

"I can see why you and your family loved it here. It's beautiful — so peaceful," she said.

"I'm sure it's a comedown from what you saw in those towering Rockies. But it's one of my special places, and, since we were so near, I wanted you to see it."

"We'll have to come back someday and hike the area more," she said. "It's beautiful."

"I'd love to show you Awosting Falls, Castle Point, Gertrude's Nose, the Palmaghatt Kill, and Awosting Lake where I went to camp as a kid. I love places like this — more so with you."

It was a wonderful day. We left Minnewaska State Park and headed for Vermont.

Later in the year Barbara and I went out of state to visit with my former church rector and his wife at his new parish, Church of Saint Mary the Virgin. We enjoyed a long and open afternoon conversation topped off with dinner and continuing talk into the late-evening hours. The next morning, Barb and I attended church next door. The interior was relatively plain and simple but spiritually enticing.

At one point before the service started, Barb leaned toward me.

"If you were to marry again, where would you want it to take place?" she quietly asked.

"I think in a church like this. How about you?" I said.

"In a beautiful outdoor setting," was her answer.

I should have guessed that and could agree. The organ pealed and the service started.

The visit with my friends only added to my strong feelings for Barbara and accented the thin ice I was on at home.

A week or so later my friend wrote:

I know how difficult *and* enhancing this time is in your life. You have been much in my thoughts and prayers since we talked. The one thing which keeps popping into my consciousness is: take time.

Regardless of relational decisions you have been opened up to live your life in a new way. Establishing that way within yourself is very important — almost without regard for marital status.

I rejoice with you in finding the new way with

all it entails in and through Barbara. I am equally
sure she has found a great deal through you. Mutu-
ality is cause for thanksgiving.

Late in the year my wife and I agreed to counseling with a
local professional who was also a former Episcopal clergy-
man and our friend. We met at the house and he asked each
of us to write out and share with him our expectations when
we were married in May 1946, and then to state our expectations now. We naturally never saw each other's responses,
but I am sure there were wide divergencies.

My own current statement was lengthy including this
excerpt:

> I want a wife–companion–best friend, all rolled into
> one, to fully share my life, to understand me, and to
> have common interests. I want someone with
> whom I can be completely open. I want and need
> an emotional outlet with a person with whom I can
> have mutual love, respect, and intimacy. . . .
> I want to live differently from here on. I want
> to live in a new way and I am still establishing that
> way within me. . . . I don't want tension. I don't
> want sorrow. I want a new life that expresses the
> real me. I know my church move is part of that
> groping for a new way of life and, frankly, a rejec-
> tion of many things that have become abhorrent to
> me. . . . I am who I am and want to be. I know my
> new lifestyle will upset my family members. I can
> only hope that understanding, love, and years will
> temper the reaction.

It was left that we would meet again, and I requested a
separate private meeting when convenient.

Life continued, and for a single semester I turned to teaching an initial course in broadcasting at the area's state college once a week. It was a new and interesting challenge with some twenty students, and we hired our first student intern at the radio station, who became an outstanding regular employee.

Life was on the fast track for me. Rationed time with Barb and outdoor activity made it bearable. I was grappling to find a way out of my dilemma. Strange, but I found that the pressures didn't affect my work. I just worked harder.

Then a welcome letter arrived from my friend:

> Your letter reflects many feelings. I rejoice for you and Barbara, your relationships, and many-faceted mutuality. Of course you are the only one who can make a decision. It certainly seems that the relationship with Barb flourishes while life with Tacy atrophies. You have every right to begin a new life, one which is yours, and expresses you.
>
> It is my feeling that God will use you more effectively in happiness than in tension and sorrow unless that tension can be worked through to some sort of health and new happiness.

In spite of my attachments, I recognized that Barbara's talents were beyond full reward in radio in her hometown. She was goal oriented and combined intelligence with a determined drive to succeed. I guess I was a mentor. In mid-1977 her interest jumped toward TV. She wrote to the general manager at Burlington's television station indicating her interests and qualifications. She eagerly waited for the response. Since I knew the general manager, I took it upon myself to write a letter highly recommending her.

In the meantime I became aware of a possible opening

at a suburban Boston television station and suggested she apply. If nothing else it would be a helpful experience. I drove her down for the appointment and interview. Nothing evolved from that meeting. She wasn't disappointed and admittedly I wasn't either for both business and personal reasons.

Barbara's growing interest in television didn't hamper her radio efforts. Her program, *The Northeast Corner*, was highly informative. It featured a full range of subjects and a variety of top-level and interesting guests. She was a good reporter and had no qualms about seeking out news stories and the people involved. She developed excellent contacts and sources from the state level down.

She was a strong writer, thorough and resourceful in her research. The subject of politics often entered our activities and conversations. Our opinions were usually in accord. Hers never interfered with objective and fair reporting.

I decided I should consult an attorney about all the legal aspects of a separation and divorce in case I decided on that course. I chose an attorney in a responsible local firm and passed over all friends in the legal profession. A lengthy meeting followed in which I explained the situation. He outlined the legal ramifications, but no steps were taken.

The Christmas season loomed just ahead. I decided to keep the lid on everything and make the holidays as enjoyable as possible for all. My daughters were coming home to be with us. On Christmas Eve we all went to the Episcopal church service.

The following week the girls were busy with friends before they returned to their respective colleges, but they became aware that something connected Barbara and me. Early one evening I went out for a walk and dropped by her place unannounced for a short time. One daughter found out and made the problem more pronounced when I returned. A difficult time ensued as the girls sensed a possible breakup of their parents' marriage. It did not add to the spirit of the season and it was untimely.

Later in the week I told my wife I needed a few days to think things over. I knew I could no longer remain under the same roof. Perhaps brazenly, but needfully, I spent New Year's Eve out of town, happily dancing the night away with Barb. There was no real decision to make. It was made. There was no turning back. I knew what I wanted. The charade was over. There was no easy way out — just a rough one with a questionable ending.

The girls went back to college and the atmosphere at home was one of quiet restraint. I knew I could no longer remain and that I should have left earlier. Late one afternoon, angry and bitter, my wife slapped my face, made disparaging remarks about a younger woman, and attributed my conduct to lust — so far from the truth that she couldn't comprehend. The incident reminded me that to this point our marriage had been devoid of physical and vocal abuse.

The encounter that afternoon brought my procrastination to an abrupt halt. I packed needed clothing, some essentials, and four of my treasured family items. I gave Corky, our cocker spaniel, a hug and a gentle pat. Stifling a few tears, I turned and left. I took one last upward glance at those towering Norway spruce trees, laden with snow, before I drove off.

I arrived at my office and sat at my desk in deep reflection. I threw my prescription bottle of Valium tablets away, vowing "Never again." I decided to turn my attention northward to the Newport area and our other station, WIKE. The dedicated manager was having a persistent health problem. The station needed more help.

It was getting dark when I drove to Barb's apartment to tell her my decision. She was helpful and understanding —

probably not totally surprised. The steak dinner hit the spot and we talked the night away. I felt relieved to be finally separated, but blamed myself for my long procrastination. I thought I had good reason, but it only complicated matters. The next morning I was bolstered by a hearty breakfast and headed some forty miles north.

I arrived in Newport, bought the local paper, saw an interesting classified ad, and followed it up. An hour later I had rented a plain, furnished, two-bedroom cottage on a sandy shoreline of beautiful Lake Memphremagog. It was winterized, furnished, well equipped, and located at the end of a winding, dead-end dirt road in Lakemont. It was made to order with its deck, front lawn, and beach area. The view was spectacular. So far, so good. I had lucked out.

Soon, Barbara received the welcome word she had been hired by the Burlington television outlet and would be trained initially as a weathercaster. She found an apartment, and on a Saturday afternoon Barbara's mother and I helped her unload and move in. She quickly became a news reporter and anchor. I was happy for her, not surprised, and felt the timing was fortunate.

The state colleges board meetings were normally held in Burlington, and I made the trip often as a trustee. One night I was really surprised to see Barbara and a television crew arrive on the scene and set up brilliant lighting fixtures. One trustee took issue and made a motion to eject the crew. Another seconded it.

Citing my role as a broadcaster as a possible conflict of interest, I said that they had every right to proceed and that we should bear any minor and temporary inconvenience caused by the lights. Others joined me and the motion was defeated with only two affirmative votes. I chuckled to myself and sent a smile to Barb. There were more important matters to consider than the bright lights.

s e v e n

More of the Same

*I love to think of nature as an unlimited broadcast-
ing station through which God speaks to us every
hour, if we will only tune in.*

GEORGE W. CARVER

I spent the required six-month separation period in my
hideaway cottage on the Canadian border. I saw Barb
more. My car burned the back roads to Burlington on our
free time and I followed her budding career on television.
On winter weekends we cross-country skied on varying land-
scapes from the twisting road at Smugglers Notch near
Stowe to the graceful forests of Bretton Woods and
Franconia, New Hampshire.

One trip took us to Mount Tremblant Regional Park near
Montreal. Never will I forget the test of my cross-country
skiing skill. We climbed to the top of a long upgrade, entering a green-and-white wondrous woodland overlooking a
pristine snow-covered lake. When I lagged behind on the
ascent, she called back to me, "Hey, ole man, almost there."
True, but the worst was yet to come. She took off, sped down
the narrow tree-lined trail on the other side, and flopped at
the bottom. With my heart pounding, and worried about
avoiding the trees on the descent, I shoved off. I made it

standing up. "Good teacher," I gasped, and she smiled.

That day at Mount Tremblant Regional Park brought home to me the sheer beauty and peace of the outdoors in winter. The air was crisp, clean, and invigorating. The evening was spent in a warm and rustic restaurant where my limited French caught a few words from neighboring tables. The good food, the roaring fire, and the red wine capped a memorable day and wonderful evening. I looked into her smiling, reddened face and sparkling eyes, and said, "Merci beaucoup, je vous aime." We were close and my world was spinning around her.

On a snowy March weekend Barb and I drove to downtown Montreal. She was covering a major parade. We worked in some sight-seeing including Vieux Montreal and the historic Notre Dame basilica. We were caught in a blizzard in Mount Royal Park overlooking the city. It was my birthday, and Barbara surprised me with two presents, both carrying strong hints — a quality pair of hiking boots and a crimson-and-white sweatsuit. Barbara loved the outdoors like no one I have ever known, and she found that same love in me.

Over the following days I sent letters to my mother, my brothers, and to my uncle (now in southern Vermont) saying, "I'm sorry for any anguish, anxiety, or misery I have caused you with my actions. You may well draw your conclusions on a strictly moral basis. Right or wrong, I think you have to consider the developmental process. Life is not cut and dry. . . . May I just say that God is forgiving . . . and perhaps in time you can be also. I stress to you that Barbara is only the trigger. The marriage counselor and others can bear this out."

Barbara and I soon made a trip to Connecticut so she could meet my older brother, Warner, and his wife, Betty. I knew a meeting with my nearby mother wasn't advisable, and that she was understandably reeling from my actions. She wasn't ready, but I was confident of the impression Barb would make that evening with my brother. A letter following our visit bore this out: "makes an excellent impression, is most attractive, highly intelligent, and mature beyond her years . . . my depth of perception runs far beyond outer appearance. Barbara passed muster on all counts, and I hope she liked us as much as we liked her." She did.

It was difficult for my mother to accept the change in my life. It was pretty clear for a time that she couldn't accept my new relationship with a young woman. I understood that natural reaction. At one point we finally talked.

"I am sorry that I have been so mean at times, but I know that you realize my dislike for certain things is inborn, and this has been hard to swallow."

"I understand fully," I said. She has never been mean.

"I want you to find the peace and happiness you want. I have put your future with Barbara in God's hands and will accept the outcome as kindly as possible. I love you dearly and your happiness is very important to me. Don't let this rough period get you down. Take good care of yourself and have faith that all will turn out for the best. I love you."

"Thanks, Mom. I love you too."

She went on at length with a number of her own astute observations on the marriage and why it had gone astray. She understood a lot more than I thought and indicated that maybe it would have been better, except for the girls, to have pulled out earlier. Her remarks cleared the air. Soon after she made a trip to Vermont to meet Barbara for the first time. The two people I admired most in this world hit it off fine. It was a good day. I was thankful and relieved. I think my mother understood.

A trial appeared unavoidable and any hopes for a settlement rapidly faded. I didn't know what to expect other than the worst. The final blow came when Tacy's attorney obtained a court subpoena ordering Barbara to appear for a deposition. She was subjected to a grueling interrogation about our relationship. I arranged to have my lawyer present. The deposition's transcript was legally harmless but personally stressful. My wife's attorney had taken the low road.

This was the final straw for me. Barbara was harmed. My only concern now was for her well-being. Maybe the intent was to scare me into a settlement — even to return to the marriage. I don't know. If so, it had the opposite effect. Utter disdain for my wife erupted within me. Barb was not the cause of the marriage breakup, but my vindictive wife was making her the scapegoat.

In early July Tacy called and summoned me to our home. She said that Melissa was planning a September marriage to the fine young man she had met in graduate school. We had met him and his parents previously. Tacy also informed me that she wanted the house painted for the occasion, a chair reupholstered, and a new car for herself. She had taken lessons and had just received her driver's license.

Quietly, I thought back over the thirty years I had served as her personal chauffeur and wondered why it had taken so long. Another car had usually been available. I was still paying all the bills, and I wished the wedding's timing was better under the circumstances. My wife outlined plans for the large wedding and reception — ideas I found extravagant. But Melissa's happiness was paramount for both of us.

Returning to Lakemont, I found a letter from our Washington broadcast attorney, Earl, acknowledging "your thoughtful letter about your move to Newport and related matters. You and your companies have been a super broadcast licensee for many, many years. . . . We hope that you have 150% degree of happiness with changes you have made and those in mind. I do not know what your feelings are about keeping the possible sale of the stations on a reasonably confidential basis, or if you plan to list with a national broker."

One night in the quiet of Lakemont I initiated the steps I would take. I contacted a respected national firm based in Atlanta to broker the sale of the radio stations. The sound advice and counsel of Art, their representative in Massachusetts, was valuable. I compiled detailed financial records, inventories, and other data to help establish sale expectations. I made some personal overtures to a few select station owners for whom I had high regard and received a few similar inquiries.

In a parallel and premature action I launched a preliminary nationwide search for a new career in either broadcasting or in the education field. My résumé was strengthened by letters of recommendation. The effort uncovered some attractive leads in both fields from Virginia, Pennsylvania, and North Carolina to Colorado, Oregon, and Arizona. All locations just happened to be in mountainous areas. I had my good and my bad days.

My uncle, Harold, called and perked me up on a down day.

"I have often wondered how you stood it so long . . . it was wonderful for you to wait until the girls were on their own, and it was a long wait." It had been.

"Barbara sounds like a gal every outdoorsman would love to have for his own to cherish. Petie and I both send our love, and our prayers will be for a happy conclusion," he added.

My mother's brother, Harold, was a lovable and amazing character, a former New York banker who took early retirement and retreated to Vermont in 1955 with his wife, Petie. I saw more of them in Vermont than as a young man in Connecticut. They had much in common including a golf craze and the love of flowers. Harold was an avid fisherman and a recognized expert at tying a fly. He liked his bourbon, and I liked his dry sense of humor.

I mentioned a standing offer I had in Virginia.

"Your new job will be a challenge, and I'm sure you will
get along with Southerners. They are really not unlike Vermonters, who look at the intrusion of outsiders as a problem. When I first came here they looked at me with a jaun-
diced eye, but when they found out I could swear as well as
or better than them I was their pal . . . when they found out
I could use a double-bitted ax, and cast a fly, I was in.

"I envy you your chance to canoe. . . . I love to hear the
paddle talk to me," he added. I guess it does.

Harold and Petie designed and supervised what is known
as the Boswell Botany Trail at the Southern Vermont Art
Center in Manchester, Vermont. This is a three-quarter mile
nature pathway lined with a good share of the known sixty-
seven varieties of Vermont ferns along with wildflowers,
plants, and trees all identified with permanent markers for
the walker. This couple's conservation of natural beauty is
still enjoyed.

A courtroom lay ahead. The six-month separation was over.
Unpleasantness was assured. My divorce filing specified "in-
tolerable severity" as the plaintiff. She immediately counter-
filed and the grind was on. The intricacies involved in the
sale of the stations were legion and complicated by new tax
laws. Other considerations abounded.

Amidst it all I had a strange but enjoyable day. Barbara
and I, her mother, father, and younger brother, drove to
Boston to see a Boston Red Sox game at Fenway Park. In
doing so I believe her folks showed extreme courtesy and
perhaps some understanding of what had transpired in our
relationship. I wondered if Harold recalled the day he contacted me about a job for his daughter. Did he regret it?

After the game we enjoyed dinner on the red-and-white
tablecloths of Durgin Park in the market area. It was an

unusual get-together and a fun day with a wonderful family. It brought back memories of a previous trip Barb and I had made to the area, including a boat tour of Boston Harbor on a choppy day and a walking tour of some historic sites.

In September 1978, I escorted my daughter Melissa down the long aisle of a crowded Catholic church. It was a beautiful wedding — a happy event. A large catered reception followed nearby. The situation was awkward with a divorce action pending, and the town was abuzz with rumors. Her plan had us at opposite ends of the long family table and of the receiving line. My younger brother rose to the occasion as a master of ceremonies, for which I was thankful. I had a happy daughter and gained a welcome son-in-law. The bride and groom departed, via Virginia, for a new home and position for John at a college in Kansas.

My mother, brothers, and their wives joined me for dinner with Barbara at a country inn on the way back to Newport. I deeply appreciated their support at the end of a busy day. It offered an opportunity for them to get to know her and to better understand our relationship. She was warmly received.

It was a certainty that my wife and her attorney would concentrate on my relationship with Barbara. Sensing the volatility and the direction things were taking, Barbara soon drove to Colorado with her mother. There she reunited with a close friend from college days. I was saddened, but fully understood. At least she was removed from the local scene and the tense situation.

I gave up any thought of remaining in the Vermont I loved so much and decided to carve my future elsewhere. The simultaneous divorce actions and negotiations on the sale of the radio stations dragged on and there was no clear end in sight. I was discouraged. My challenging six-year term on the state colleges board was coming to an end and I severed all my other positions and connections with other organizations so I could concentrate on these matters, my regular work responsibilities, and my future plans.

The peace and quiet of my Lakemont refuge helped to accomplish this. My canoe often plied the jagged shoreline of the lake. I took my frustrations out on the tennis courts at Jay Peak in a weekly men's group and switched to cross-country ski trails there on winter weekends.

New friendships from other walks of life provided a needed lift, and Shirley and Doug, a young married couple, became special to me. I knew that old friends tend to fade away during a divorce lest they show any favoritism.

In December, Barbara returned home for Christmas and we made arrangements to meet again — on Christmas Eve. We met at her parents' home in central Vermont. Her parents had gone to church. Her younger brother was home. Our meeting was warm and only rekindled feelings. We retreated outside to my car, and I warmed her with the gift of a needed long winter coat and a final embrace. That evening was the bright light of my holiday period. However, given the circumstances, it was difficult for both of us.

The next afternoon I arrived at my older brother's home in Connecticut. I knew my mother was staying with them, bedridden, and that she had no desire to rise. That was very much out of line for her. I suspected that my own troubled life was at least a contributing factor, and that she was despondent. My brother had hinted at this.

I leaned down, planted a kiss on her cheek, clasped her hand, and talked privately.

"Mom, this is no place to be on Christmas. Let me just say that you have always been the one who never looked back, and always forged ahead. You said on more than one occasion to me just keep going in life — what's past is past."

Her eyes were directly on me and a small smile crept over her face, but she was silent.

The words came slowly from my lips. "Mom. I'm okay. I'm confident I'm on the right course and that things will work out. I now have some of that strong faith that I've seen in your life. I won't forget your granddaughters, and I will do what is necessary for my wife. I love you very much, and I'm sorry for any concerns relating to me.

"I have the will to work things out now and in the future. Honestly, I'm excited. As for you, you just need the will to get better now. We all need you."

The smile was better. A few words followed. I held her hand, kissed her wrinkled forehead, and retreated from the darkened room with a prayer in my heart.

The next day I returned to Lakemont, and was soon informed by my brother that my mother had made a quick recovery and was up and around. I thanked Him.

In March I gave an interview to a Vermont Press Bureau reporter at my office in St. Johnsbury. It was on the eve of my exit as a trustee of the Vermont State Colleges. I took issue with Governor Snelling's charge that the chancellor, trustees, and college officials were to blame for the financial crisis facing the state colleges.

The press report quoted me as saying "public higher education in Vermont just plain hasn't had the support it has had in other states. No single chancellor and no single board should be blamed for the crisis. It has just been a case over the years of being lean and ill . . . you take desperate measures."

The governor blasted the trustees and college officials for not scaling down operations or raising tuitions to cut the colleges' operating deficit. The House Appropriations Committee sought to cut funding for Vemont Community College, putting its future in jeopardy.

Newspapers quoted me as saying that the basic problem had been to keep a badly needed system of colleges going without adequate funding. They reported that I didn't blame anyone specifically but noted that governors and legislatures had consistently failed to provide adequate money for the Vermont State Colleges.

The newspaper article on the interview ended with a quote: "Years ago I used to think that education was above politics, but now I know it's right smack in the middle of politics." It was. It is. It will be.

In early 1979 I flew to Colorado to spend time with Barbara. She met me at the Denver airport. I rented a car, checked into a nearby motel, and moved the next morning to one in Boulder. She took me sight-seeing. A few days later we flew to Casper, Wyoming, where she was interviewed for an opening at a major radio station. Casper surprised me, with its maze of oil rigs against the snow-covered mountains.

Back in Colorado the visit was capped with dinner at a country inn high up in the hills. It was a storybook setting. I sensed this evening would be our last for a long time. Maybe forever? Freshly fallen snow covered bending tree limbs, and the inn was partially buried. Icy windows trimmed its front. Once we were inside, the glow and smell of a huge log fire created warmth.

The conversation was relaxed and quiet. Our paths had crossed again, but we were leaning in different directions now. I didn't spoil the evening with details of my difficult pending divorce. She had suffered enough stress of her own. We did reshare good times together.

"Barb," I said, "you are truly my best friend and I have more in common with you than anyone I've ever known. I love you for all you mean to me, come what may." She was always so outspokenly natural and radiant with her magnetic smile, her dimples, and sparkling eyes. It was a memorable evening.

"Where will you go if you leave Vermont?" she asked.

"I'm not sure yet. I have some irons in the fire in Virginia and elsewhere — even Oregon. I have to wrap things up first."

"Where are you headed from here?" she added.

"I fly to Dallas for a meeting of broadcasters. I have some appointments and hope to add some contacts that may be helpful too."

"Well, I'll leave here for Wyoming if the job comes through, and I hope it does," she said.

"It will, Barb, and you'll do fine. Thanks for a wonderful time again. Ours is a very special relationship. Others, except for a few, find it hard to even imagine. Life goes on, Barb. We both relish it and we both will make it," I looked straight into her blue eyes.

Our farewell the next morning at her place was warm, yet tinged with sadness. I took her in my arms, kissed her, and flew off to Dallas full of Barbara memories.

I accomplished what I set out to do in Dallas. I added a visit to the site where President Kennedy met the tragic end to his life. The Kennedy mystique was still with me. Back in Vermont, I received word from Barbara. She was moving to Casper.

It was crunch time. After rejecting offers from commercial broadcasters, some of whom I knew well, I accepted a firm offer from two younger Boston-based ophthalmologists who owned radio stations in northern California, Colorado, and Wyoming. They came to visit the stations and I was genuinely impressed. Our conversations were rewarding and their plans acceptable. They met and were equally impressed by our key employees, and indicated that no staff changes would occur. Doug, who swept the floors as a high school student, had become an announcer, then program director, and was now a station manager. All were hardworking, dedicated, and highly qualified.

Brent and Eric were Mormons originally from Utah. I recalled my Mormon friends in the service and the high regard I had for their standards and ethics. I sensed the same qualities in these two personable and competent young gentlemen. I believed it was in the best interest of the stations, and negotiations reached a successful conclusion weeks later. It was a solid, sound decision and also key to the stalled divorce proceedings.

My wife's attorney made an attempt to hold up the sale of the stations until she obtained legal claim to an equal portion of the escrow funds deposited to seal the transactions. It was an ugly interruption and my attorney stressed strong legal action would follow if they interfered with the sale or jeopardized it in any way.

On June 12, stockholders were advised of the execution of a sales contract for 100 percent of the stock of both companies and were advised about the necessary transfers. All were accomplished in reasonable time. The extensive negotiations, the accumulation of many documents, and the massive amount of paperwork took a lot of time, but I was relieved. The sale now hinged on the application to the Federal Communications Commission for approval of the sale, and I was confident.

A reporter for the *Burlington Free Press,* the state's largest newspaper, once wrote an article that said: "With twenty dollars left in the checkbook, a sublime faith in his adopted Vermont, and quite a lot of gall, a twenty-six-year-old veteran who literally had no experience in the field started a radio station in St. Johnsbury. . . . The story of the young man's venture into business in Vermont belies the claim young people cannot get ahead in the Green Mountain State.

His success was not a matter of falling into a streak of luck, but of sticking with an idea he thought could work, and having faith in the people surrounding him."

I thought the last six words really told the story. Thirty exciting years rolled over in my mind, and an unknown future took hold. Hope for an out-of-court divorce settlement was out the window. It was now in the hands of a neutral and, I hoped, fair-minded judge in a courtroom.

I turned all my attention to finding a job in a good location in broadcast management and sales, or possibly in the field of education at the college level. I did apply for a position as an assistant to the president of a university in Oregon, and survived the process for a while. I finally decided to accept a job in Virginia as the general manager of a radio station in an attractive small city with the prospect of buying in.

eight

Retreat South

Who ne'er has suffered,
he has lived but half.
He never failed, he never
strove or sought.
Who never wept is stranger
to a laugh.
And he who never doubted,
never thought.

REV. J. B. GOODE

The day came for the confrontation in the old red-brick county courthouse a few blocks from our home. It was time to resolve matters in a legal forum. I felt genuinely composed as I entered the building and spotted the cordial county clerk who had handled office duties at the radio station for a number of years.

I strode into the spacious courtroom and joined my attorney. With a quick glance off to one side I noted my wife conferring with her legal counsel and also the presence of my two daughters. We were soon joined by the judge and a stenographer and the trial got underway.

My wife's attorney called a certified public accountant to the stand. He testified that he had thoroughly examined the accounting records of the stations. The crux of his testimony was that I was capable of drawing a much larger salary than I was, making reference to cash assets available.

My testimony took direct issue and indicated that such assets were being preserved to help underwrite pending plans for a frequency modulation companion radio station. An application was on file with the government. I further stated that my first responsibilities were to the stockholders. Inside I was at a slow burn, but that didn't show. What next?

My wife's attorney produced a number of small checks made out to Barbara and asked me what they were for. They were innocuous, and included some to help on her car expenses for work. She was on her own with a limited income. She had offered remuneration. No, I never paid any rent, as she said in her deposition. His rapid interrogation naturally accented my relationship with a young woman, but there was no evidence presented of overnight wrongdoing or the like. It was all speculation.

Now and then a few unknown strangers would walk in the rear doors, sit down, and take in the show. I knew a friend and client of mine along with his wife were in an adjacent waiting room, subpoenaed by my wife's attorney. I sensed they were probably uncomfortable, and I was sorry that they were involved. I knew what was coming.

That knowledge led to an automatic decision and a few words with my attorney. I simply wanted to clear the air, make an honest, forthright statement, and bring to an end the incessant bitter verbal insinuations involving Barbara. I did just that to the court.

"I just want to say that I consider Barbara to be my best friend and I admit to having an intimate relationship with her." I provided no details. Webster's definition of *intimate* fit.

My good friend, with a slight grin and ruffled hair, slowly shuffled to the stand.

"Did you observe the plaintiff and a young woman on New Year's Eve? . . . Can you tell us where?" the lawyer asked.

My friend sheepishly answered the question, saying, "Yes, we saw them in a Burlington hotel."

"Where in the hotel did you observe them and what were they doing?" snapped the lawyer as he moved closer to the witness.

"They were just dancing like everyone else and obviously having a wonderful time," my friend testified. There were a few smiles. It was plainly revealed that this was the only time and place we had been seen despite the veiled inference by the attorney.

My two daughters joined me for a lunch break at a local restaurant and we talked about other things. Inside I agonized over their presence at the trial, which could have been avoided with an out-of-court settlement.

The young, competent opposing attorney built his case on trying to show that his client's full-time raising of the children at home equaled my financial contribution to the marriage. He called my younger daughter to the stand to provide some detail. When she concluded I asked my attorney to go easy and pose only one simple direct question, which he did.

"Was your father a good father?"

"Yes," was the firm answer, as I knew it would be.

It was an understandably uncomfortable occasion for all involved. It could have been much worse. I refrained from addressing the real reasons for the breakdown of the marriage. It wasn't caused by a young woman in 1976. That only triggered the final impetus for ending a relationship that had been unhappy for many years.

Only a few people knew the real problems and the reason I had not left sooner. I was determined to hang in and fulfill my responsibilities throughout the college years of our two beloved daughters.

I left the courtroom relieved and didn't share the bitterness I knew raged within my wife. She was a good woman but vindictive now. I was sorry, but we were not meant for each other. I was fully prepared to give her the beautiful home we had shared along with our fine joint furnishings. I expected her to be given very substantial proceeds from the sale of the stations. The final overall settlement was now in the hands of the court.

When the date was set for the closing on the sale of the radio stations I drove to Virginia to make arrangements for my move there. I found a two-bedroom town house near a college in Harrisonburg and purchased basic furniture for later delivery. I noted the inviting swimming pool and tennis courts on the premises and returned to Vermont.

The closing on the sale of the stations took place in the law offices of the purchasers' attorney in Montpelier, the state capital, on September 13, 1979. Luckily it was over quickly. There were handshakes all around and warm parting words. At age fifty-five I ended my Vermont broadcasting career. I left for Lakemont with a lump in my throat and a check in my hand, deep in thought and excited about the new life waiting for me in the Shenandoah Valley of Virginia. Life goes on by your making. I was ready.

I arranged a good-bye get-together and dinner at the Landing, a restaurant on the lakeshore where I often had paddled my canoe. It was an unusual mix of some fifty friends and others in the area with whom I had been associated for almost two years. All had touched my life in some meaningful way for which I was appreciative. They ranged from professionals to a hippie-type young couple; from ski bums to some now former staff members, and just plain Vermonters.

The scene was special, with a sweeping view through the

picture windows of the lake and distant mountains. One person noted the unusual mix of people in attendance and wondered how I had met them all. That would be a book in itself. They were a group of fine human beings from all walks of life.

The party atmosphere quieted down when I ended the evening with a few chosen words:

"I will never forget my radio days in Vermont or the days I have spent here on the shores of this beautiful lake — or all of you. Vermont has been a special place to live and work and raise a family. I am thankful that I found my way here more than thirty years ago, but it's time for me to get on with life somewhere else. . . . Good friends are essential for a good life. Thank you for everything and for being here tonight. 'Til we meet again" — and I raised my glass to all of them.

The next day I drove to Burlington and bought a new small Buick. I added a hitch and packed a small U-Haul the following day. That last evening I sat in the easy chair and disjointed thoughts filtered through my mind. I agonized, but my personal situation only accented the need to sell and move on. I thought of the peace and happiness I had found at Lakemont.

The divorce settlement was now in the judge's hands. I know from real experience that divorce has tragic consequences for the principals and their families. My grown daughters experienced sadness, deep concern, and insecurity. They logically attributed the breakup to Barbara, completely unaware of my long-subdued feelings. There was initial anger. They found it incredulous. They were so wrong — understandably so. I know that love should be looking out for the interests and happiness of others and certainly your daughters. I tried.

I thought of my wife. I regretted that my marriage fell

apart. It ran out of steam. We had few common denominators, lacked spark, and never discovered passion. We were two different people. We didn't communicate enough. Our interests were different. We didn't support each other's activities enough.

I thought of Barb. We had just about everything in common except our ages. I admired her way of life, her natural behavior and openness. She was one of a kind — my kind. No, she wasn't perfect. No one is. She could at times be independent, outspoken, critical, and even aloof, but we could always talk things out.

I turned to my counselor-friend's letter before calling it a day. "You must love your neighbor as yourself. God doesn't want our facade or outer shell. He wants all of us. . . . I'm convinced you are very willing to be broken open and made new. . . . Don't let the false cross of conventional morality deter you from bearing your own true cross and becoming a new being. Worldly wisdom tends to discount this Truth because the ways of the world are not the ways of God." I read his words over and over.

The next morning I rose early and headed for my mother's home in Connecticut on the first leg of the trip to Virginia. I went down I-91 with mountain scenery looming on both sides of the Connecticut River. Mountains make me think, make me wonder and feel good. They are a vivid reminder that "in the beginning God created the heavens and the earth." They beat man's skyscrapers towering over crowded asphalt city streets.

I arrived at my mother's home and spent a relaxed evening and enjoyed a favorite home-cooked meal. Afterward we talked about everything. I sensed she was concerned about my future, but relieved that I had settled on Virginia.

We talked about some of our trips together. We talked about the bus tours she had made on her own: to Banff

National Park and Lake Louise in Alberta Province, Canada, to the Smokies in recent years.

"What about your recent trip across the Atlantic? How did that ever come about?" I asked.

"Well, I'd never flown, but decided to spread my wings when my old friend Gertrude invited me to her home in Paris," she said. "Her husband, who had a diplomatic job, is no longer living. We have corresponded. I just couldn't turn down the opportunity, so my first plane flight took me across the Atlantic. We toured France, Italy, and even drove up into the Alps in her little open sports car. It was wonderful. We saw so much for a couple of old geezers!" Her face lit up. I saw the spark was still there.

"That's a little different from our train trip to California some years ago," I said.

"I wouldn't say that. Seeing the Grand Canyon as we did has always been a highlight — still is. Guess it whetted my appetite for seeing more in my lifetime."

"Good, I'm glad for that," I said.

"I know you have your apartment. Don't you need dishes and all those other housekeeping items? Is your place furnished?" she asked.

"Oh, I'm in good shape with furniture and bedding. I'll make out okay. I do have a new set of dishes in the U-Haul. I'll show them to you."

I went outside and returned with a box containing a complete set of attractive white Royal Staffordshire dishes.

"Beautiful — good taste," she said. "What store did you find them in?"

"I didn't. I got them on my credit card through a special offering from Mobil. I thought it was a neat deal for the price."

"My goodness, they're lovely. You are resourceful."

"Mom, you taught me a lot of things. I owe you so much

and I have to admit I owe my army training a little something too. I make a tight, very neat bed," I said with a chuckle. "I'll even give you a good home-cooked meal when you come down to visit — better than those Sunday night suppers I used to get here at home when you made popcorn in the fireplace."

Mom retreated to the kitchen to turn off the whistling tea kettle. I glanced around the living room looking at all the family pictures, soaking up old times. She returned with tea and some molasses cookies and the conversation turned to family.

"I am so glad things are straightening out for you and that you can get on with your life after these bumpy years. I feel much better about all that has happened."

"Thanks, Mom. Things will work out for everyone."

"I know Tacy is hurt and jealous for which you cannot blame her. . . . I know you will do whatever is necessary for her care."

"That goes without saying — what's necessary."

"You have done all a father could be called upon to do — and more. . . . I never heard her say I am sorry to keep you waiting, which I admit was due hundreds of times . . . the telephone, which she has horribly abused . . . You were too patient many times when you should have told her where to get off. The girls are innocent victims and have much to be grateful to you for, carrying on until they were out on their own even if it might have been better for both you and Tacy to have separated earlier."

"Looking back I believe it would have been better all the way around, but that's all hindsight. Only the future lies ahead," I said.

"What about Barbara?" she asked.

"I don't know. Only time will tell. Our lives are on courses far apart now. I will never forget her, come what may. We

shared a lot. At least she gave me the best years of my life —
in some ways the worst too," I said.

It was a valuable evening. I was heartened by my mother's
words and her indomitable spirit. I slept soundly.

The next morning I was up and away after a hearty breakfast and final words with my mother. I was a little concerned
about the occasional sways of the U-Haul as I headed south
to the Shenandoah Valley, and felt strangely at ease when I
finally saw a WELCOME TO VIRGINIA sign on I-81.

I arrived at the town house complex in Harrisonburg in
the late afternoon. My furniture had already been delivered
and was in place. A quick shopping tour added some essentials and groceries. I turned on the radio station I was going
to manage, and then monitored some competitive stations.

I explored the area the next morning and my initial im-
pressions proved sound. It was attractive, enhanced by a
number of colleges, an eighty-store indoor mall, and a balanced economy. There were seven radio stations in the county
area, an ABC television station, and a major daily newspaper. The outlook was competitive and my work was cut out
for me.

The next day I met with Wally, the owner, to talk over
my assumption of management and participation in the ownership. He was a true Southern gentleman of the old style
— courteous and gracious. He was born and raised in West
Virginia's coal mine country. Wally was a former University
of Miami football player and boxer and looked it, with a
large muscular frame indicating he wasn't one to tangle with.
Wally had inherited substantial wealth and amassed more
raising and selling chinchillas before the market disappeared.
Now he played with his radio station, watched the stock
market, and clipped coupons.

He was an eligible bachelor who, once terribly disappointed in love, never married. He knew and loved horses,

and he was a good horse show judge. He was a devout conservative Republican of the Goldwater type and a Ronald Reagan enthusiast. He loved to get going on politics, but I knew enough not to chime in.

I spent the early days in overall management and a heavy personal sales effort. Two longtime key employees clearly frowned on my presence. My discovery of some skimming and trade deals, and shaking up sales-account assignments didn't endear me to them either. We had our own little civil war. The advent of more full-time radio competition in the market complicated our sales.

I turned north to help solve the problems and hired three of my former Vermont employees to bolster the operation. All were solid experienced announcers and one had an extensive sales background too. Programming was expanded in music, news, sports, public service, and promotional efforts. Close ties were initiated with nearby schools and colleges including James Madison University with its ten thousand students. However, daytime operation from sunrise to sunset, even with more power, proved to be a problem when competing with full-time competitors.

My mother, older brother, and his wife arrived on a lovely late October day to check on me. I'm sure they were concerned about my ability to set up house and fend for myself in a new environment. They were soon convinced otherwise and impressed with my progress: the comfortable town house, the city and surroundings. They were not impressed with Virginia's fall foliage the next day. It was obscured by a freak snowstorm of blizzard proportions. They sat in a motel without power on a late October day, but had a brief tour of the area before happily returning home.

I rejoined Kiwanis, which I had belonged to for twenty-five years in Vermont. I played tennis in a men's group two nights a week and worked myself into good physical shape.

I socialized with some of the television staff. I dated an attractive woman who worked at the local cable television company. I enjoyed the hospitality of a widow at a party but dropped her after I survived a surprise private candlelight dinner at her home. I was purposely elusive, worn out by divorce.

There was an unexpected exception. An old Washington and Lee friend learned of my move and invited me to dinner at his home in a nearby city. I accepted and he met me at the front door when I arrived. We shook hands.

"Let's go in the living room. I want you to meet someone else we invited," he said with a broad smile as he escorted me down the hall.

I noted his pretty wife, Helen, and another attractive woman sitting on the couch in the living room.

"Oh, my gosh, Ann, I don't believe it. It's great to see you after all these years — more than thirty I'm sure. What a fine surprise."

I quickly learned that her husband had passed on some years ago. Both he and his brother went to Washington and Lee. We all had lived in the same four-family apartment house when my wife and I returned after the war. A heart-warming evening followed with old friends.

Ann and I followed up in the months that followed with some dates including dinner at her home, a visit with a Vermont friend of mine and his wife near Lexington, and a return to a class reunion at college. Spring brought a return visit from my mother, older brother, and his wife, and they met Ann at lunch in a scenic restaurant atop the Blue Ridge Mountains before a visit to nearby Monticello, Thomas Jefferson's historic estate. Ann made a real impression and I'm sure my family speculated on my relationship with this very pretty and outgoing Southern woman. She was more my age.

I would get a little bored and lonely at times. My remedy was a nostalgic trip back to Lexington — usually including a visit to Goshen Pass, my favorite spot in all Virginia, just west on beautiful Route 39. It is a sure reminder of the similar Route 100 that runs the length of Vermont.

The rocky bed of the Maury River flows through the long twisting pass and stretches for miles. Stone-faced mountains with towering trees look down on the peaceful setting free of the touches of men. Fall adds a patchwork of bright colors. College students often partied there. Fishermen tried their luck. Goshen Pass is even more fascinating in the dead of winter when its face is masked with snow.

In late March 1980 I received a copy of the judgment order finalizing my divorce. The settlement, as expected, was heavily weighted in my former wife's favor. It gave her our "large residence" with a very minimal mortgage encumbrance along with the substantial furnishings and appliances. It provided for ten years of substantial alimony payments, and "as additional alimony" I was to provide medical insurance and/or pay all uninsured medical and hospital expenses.

The judgment made reference to the fact that my wife "has no training or experience for employment . . . suffers from painful degenerative arthritis of the knees and feet." It went on to say she "may require a leg alignment operation in the future and may ultimately be confined to a wheelchair in ten to fifteen years."

It also indicated "the marriage began to fail as early as 1967 and had substantially ended by the middle of the seventies," and that I became "involved in a personal relationship with a woman employee from 1976 to 1978."

The judgment indicated she "should receive property and a share of the proceeds from the sale of the station at least sufficient to maintain her at a standard of living close to her present standard of living for the foreseeable future (whether in her present large home or in another smaller home or apartment) and sufficient to pay her income taxes on the alimony." I had honored my financial responsibilities to her from the start and continued. I did feel the overall award was excessive, but it was more water over the dam. Life goes on.

The year ahead found me recovering from the wounds of divorce. Good news arrived that my older daughter, her husband, and newly born Jennifer were moving to Pennsylvania. Soon after, my daughter flew east and I met her in Harrisburg. We found an apartment in nearby Carlisle, home of Dickinson College, where John successfully sought a library position. We had a fine reunion.

I made a special trip back to the Vermont area to visit my younger daughter who was now working as a social director in a health and extended care facility in Hanover, New Hampshire. I found her spirits raised and was thankful. She seemed fine, but I knew she often kept things to herself. It was good to be with her again.

I attended a national radio programming conference in New Orleans and met Larry King doing a late-night radio talk show in the hotel lobby. I met a suave talkative Jim Garrison in a local restaurant. He was the New Orleans district attorney who advanced a conspiracy theory on the assassination of Robert Kennedy. The captivating conversation again refueled my continuing interest in the Kennedy mystique.

I went to meet family members at a favorite place on Lake Morey in central Vermont. I arrived late in the afternoon the day before for a special reason unbeknownst to others — to meet Barbara. She had come east with a girlfriend to visit her parents in Vermont for a few days and to climb Mount Washington.

Barb and her friend arrived in a small pickup truck loaded

with gear. She was dressed in blue jeans, had that same captivating smile, and we embraced warmly. She looked great and I liked her sidekick. We talked some and then retreated to, yes — a tennis court for another go. I took them both on in a real ding-dong battle and won. Barb and I had the chance to talk more when we retreated to a waterfront deck for coffee. It seemed like old times, but I knew they were new. Old feelings lingered when she left for her parents' home.

That afternoon my mother, older brother, and sister-in-law arrived for several nights. Shirley and her husband, a couple I had befriended in Newport, dropped by and stayed overnight. The evening was spent in competition at a pool table. My mother and Shirley turned out to be the sharpshooters and shamed us. It was a fun evening with family and two close friends. It was good to be back in Vermont.

Back home, I plunged into long hours at work. I drew some enjoyment from guest teaching a class in broadcast management at Washington and Lee. I hired a journalism student for a two-month period as a news intern at the station. His writing ability was greater than his performance. He became a newspaper sports reporter in his first job, but then jumped to the White House where he was responsible for compiling an overnight summary of pertinent news gleaned from media. The report was placed on the president's desk for his morning arrival. I am sure it was well prepared. He was a talented journalism graduate.

As I settled back into a routine, I found myself looking for something to do one Saturday night. The movies didn't appeal to me. I caught an item in the local paper that Parents Without Partners was sponsoring a dance in a hall just north of the city. I drove out to the site, balked, and headed home, and then for some reason went back, determined to go in.

I bought a ticket at the entrance and noticed an attractive

woman selling them. A good crowd was divided between the dance floor and sitting at tables scattered around the hall. I found a place to sit down and soon accepted an invitation to dance from a woman across the way.

We danced just once. My eyes continually lighted on the pretty ticket taker in the gold dress. She was more my type. I took a chance and went over to her.

"Hi, I know you're selling tickets, but there seems to be a lull. Would you like to dance?" I said.

"Sure, I'd like to," she answered, asking an associate to cover her.

We hit the crowded dance floor during a slow number. I had planned that not knowing her preference, but aware of mine.

"What's your name? Are you from here?" I asked.

"I'm Elaine and I'm from Harrisonburg. How about you?"

I gave her my name and told her I lived in Harrisonburg too.

"Do you often come to these affairs?" I asked.

"Now and then. I had a date, but he called saying he was under the weather so I volunteered to help sell tickets. How about you?"

"No date. I'm single, just recently moved here, and I really drifted in for something to do tonight. Do you work?" I said.

"I've been teaching English to slow learners at a local high school, but I'm going to school locally to become a professional hairstylist. I want to open my own hairstyling shop here. What do you do?"

"I'm the manager of a local radio station," and I explained.

The conversation went on as we danced the night away. She never went back to selling tickets. We were both divorced and she had three sons. She explained that she lived with her youngest son, Troy, thirteen. The two older sons

lived locally with their father, a college athletics coach. She
had been divorced for about three years. I surmised I was
about fifteen years older and she probably did too. I was
graying. She had a striking head of blond hair.

I was taken with her appearance at the very outset. I
became even more attracted when we talked. She was not
only extremely attractive, but obviously natural, outgoing,
and intelligent. Her sense of humor was good too. Our dancing meshed just fine. We just plain hit it off and enjoyed the
time there.

"Would you like to come by my place for a cup of coffee
before you head back? You can just follow me there."

"Okay, I'd like to," I replied with no hesitation.

We arrived at an attractive brick split-level on a hillside
a short distance from a college campus. I followed her into
an apartment that covered the entire lower floor, overlooking the valley below. It was plain and neat.

We sat and talked over coffee in the spacious comfortable
living room. The long conversation revealed that she was born
in Iowa and had lived in Colorado, Nebraska, and Oregon.
She had been raised in a struggling and strict Mennonite
family. Her father, now deceased, had been a pastor in churches
of that faith, and her mother helped him. He also worked as
a contractor. Her mother was now in Oregon.

"My folks sent me to a Mennonite junior college in Kansas, and I graduated from there," she said. "I guess they just
wanted me to continue in my narrow heritage and not get
out of line. Couldn't dance like we did tonight — couldn't
do a lot of things. It was strict. Things were kind of tough
economically for us too."

"How long have you been here in Virginia?"

"Oh, sixteen years I guess. I married a guy from Oregon
and we finally moved here. He's the soccer and wrestling
coach at the college. I went back to college and got my

degree here when I was thirty-seven. We lived high in the mountains of northern India for about three years when the boys were young. As a matter of fact, Troy, the youngest who lives with me now, was born in New Delhi." She showed me a picture.

"What ever took you to India of all places?" I asked.

"We were really Mennonite missionaries. My husband taught in a school there associated with World Vision. I helped in some areas. It was a great experience. Our return to the states was delayed for a month when I was hospitalized with hepatitis. I was so sick and so disappointed."

"How did you get it?" I asked.

"I don't really know exactly, but human squalor and unhealthy conditions were common there. Animals everywhere added to the unsanitary picture too. Women would crowd the shores of the river washing clothes in the already murky water and kids would swim and play in it."

"What about drinking water?" I asked. "That could do it."

"We were okay at the school. I don't know how I got it. We even had a native servant who helped around the house — for next to nothing. She was lovely. We still stay in touch."

The conversation went back and forth and we both added more details about our lives. She noted she was now living in a predominantly Mennonite neighborhood and that her ex-husband and two older sons lived just a few blocks away.

"I gather your ex-husband is a very religious person," I said.

"Yes, but divorce is naturally frowned on and makes it difficult for both of us in the Mennonite community now."

"Did you and your husband work out the divorce amiably?"

"No, I had a real battle to get custody of my youngest son, and thank God I got him," she said as she rose to turn off the outside light.

She looked lovely but I caught a few yawns.

"I think I'd better get going. I appreciate the good time this evening. It's been fun."

"It's awfully late and raining hard now. Look, you're welcome to stay here tonight and sleep here in the living room. The couch is comfortable," she said.

"Thanks but I'm not sure that's a good idea. I'm not sure your son would appreciate it either."

"Troy won't be back tonight. He's down with his brothers at their father's house," she said. "It's okay."

"Well, all right, I will," I said, feeling comfortable with the invitation, tired, and looking at the mantel clock.

"No problem, you're welcome — and for breakfast. It's been a nice evening."

"But your date never showed," I said.

"I'm glad he didn't," she said with a smile. "Get some rest. I'll let you know when the coffee is on in the morning. Good night," and she headed for her bedroom at the other end of the long living room.

It was an unexpected and unusually nice evening. It sure beat watching television by myself at home. She was just plain nice. I wondered where I was headed as I quickly dozed off as the rain spattered on the windows.

nine

Here We Go Again

*Let us never forget that an act of goodness is of itself
an act of happiness. No reward coming after the
event can compare with the sweet reward that went
with it.*

MAURICE MAETERLINK

In the days that followed Elaine and I became good friends and I had an opportunity to meet Troy, her youngest. I took an immediate liking to him. He was a good-looking lad, tanned, with blond hair. His smile was contagious. He was courteous. I wondered what was floating through his mind as he tried to size me up. I had no problem. I had never had a son, but sensed she had a good one.

Elaine and I continued to see each other, take in a movie, go for a drive, or dine out. One evening she invited me for dinner with Troy and Todd, her middle son. Todd was a handsome high school student with black hair and a muscular build, and I suspected that he was the envy of every guy in the school.

I believe it was difficult for Todd to meet his mother's new friend. His conversation was restrained, but courteous. Things hit home near the end of the meal. Todd rose without a word and departed. I felt it, but didn't fault him. I could understand. I wondered about meeting Eric, a college student.

In the weeks ahead Florence, Elaine's widowed mother, came east to live nearby. She was short, bright, and a warm individual, highly self-educated and deeply religious. She had been raised in a poor family of nine and had gone out on her own at an early age. I liked her immediately. She had a touch of grace about her. She was a fabulous quilt maker and an exceptional cook. She genuinely enjoyed saying grace at mealtime. Her words were lengthy, almost poetic, but the food could get cold.

Elaine and I cheered for Troy and Todd on soccer fields and wrestling mats. We covered Virginia watching Troy roll up a statewide wrestling reputation and championship. He was light, agile, and tough. He wouldn't give up. Both boys were standouts on a soccer field. Eric, the oldest son, was more reserved, studious, and buried his energies in books and computers at the nearby college. All three were exceptional, clean-cut young men with high standards. They were good students. Elaine and her ex-husband had done something right.

Life picked up for me. Elaine and I had similar interests. We played some tennis. We enjoyed some trips to Myrtle Beach with Troy and a buddy. We grew a large vegetable garden behind her house, and her mother taught me to shuck corn. We tended grapevines and flower beds. It was good to mow a lawn again. We attended high school events and witnessed Todd's acting ability on stage. We attended the campus Mennonite church initially but quickly turned to an Episcopal church. We were both divorced and this made it awkward in the former, although the pastor was kind. The change was radical for Elaine.

Elaine successfully launched Elaine's Hairstyling, leasing store space in the heart of the small city. Elaine, her

mother, and I wielded paint brushes and floor mops in preparation. Equipment for three styling stations arrived, and her
decorating skills created an attractive salon. I took on her
accounting chores at no charge. Elaine and her two young
stylists piled in the customers, including lots of James Madison University coeds.

Her natural public relations flair, hard work, and sales
ability paid off. She won recognition as the number one student in a large Dale Carnegie Course class. The competition was based on presence, content, and delivery of prepared material. I witnessed her successful effort and easily
agreed with the judges.

My work at the radio station was challenging, but we
were a daytimer up against full-time radio stations in the
market. I was concerned about the long road. I became a
professional member of a journalism fraternity at the university, and was involved in chamber of commerce and tour-
ism activities along with Kiwanis.

One day I received a short letter from Marie, a stockholder in my first Vermont radio station. She had invested
one thousand dollars and when the station was sold received
more than thirty-eight thousand dollars as well as a divi-
dend check every year. The check was timely as she encountered both health problems and retirement years. I'm sure
she was surprised.

"I deeply appreciate what you have done for me and the
rest of us. I am just beginning to realize to some little extent
what the whole job must have entailed. Thank God for you
and may He bless you always."

I appreciated her help in making my initial effort in Vermont possible. I felt good. She made my day.

In April 1981 I flew back to Vermont to join with family and attend the funeral of my uncle. Harold, my mother's
brother, was a friendly outgoing character who had left

banking and the sidewalks of New York City for the country charm of Vermont. He was the consummate outdoorsman, full of stories, and at ease tying trout flies and paddling his canoe. His wife had traded selling high-priced real estate in Greenwich, Connecticut, for protecting it in Vermont as a naturalist and environmentalist. They were quite a pair. He was easygoing. She could be tough at a bridge table or spending a dollar. She had a soft side too.

Uncle Harold never played any real role in my boyhood days in Greenwich, nor did his wife, Petie. He never plugged in after my dad died. He lived with his mother until he married in later years. Our paths really crossed when we both became Vermonters. I sensed that my mother and Petie didn't have a close relationship — perhaps they had a strained one — and that may be the reason we never saw them much when I lived in Connecticut.

I came to know my uncle in Vermont. He experienced multiple operations, but always came up smiling. He liked a touch of bourbon, which loosened his tongue for a few cuss words about Democrats. He found peace in the handiwork of nature and the animals that roamed it. He was a golf addict and talented amateur painter. I will always remember sitting with him on his porch one afternoon when a hummingbird alighted and remained on his shoulder. He was a good guy, had a humorous spark. I smile when I think of him.

In the summer I took Elaine to my mother's Connecticut home for dinner and overnight. Mother was relaxed, kind, and courteous. I am sure underneath she wondered about this new relationship and where it was headed. She probably drew her own initial comparison to my former wife. I believe any concerns were dispelled in the long conversation over dinner and after. Elaine received an even warmer introduction from my older brother and his wife who lived nearby.

I gave Elaine a brief tour of my old hometown — where

I was born, went to school and church, played tennis, and went swimming. She was naturally impressed by the visual beauty and unusual wealth of Greenwich, but I stressed that I had left it early on, by choice.

We continued on to Vermont for a complete tour of the area where I had lived for thirty-two years. It was like a trip into the past for me, but it turned us both to the future. We stopped at a small jewelry store run by a friend. We walked in holding hands. We left smiling, Elaine wearing a beautifully crafted diamond engagement ring. We returned to Virginia, and to work.

Later in the year my mother flew to Charlottesville and joined me for a few days. I took her on a tour of Warm Springs and the famous Homestead at Hot Springs where her brother, Harold, had spent his honeymoon. We stayed at her favorite motel, the Keydet-General in Lexington. The next day we went sight-seeing on the Blue Ridge Parkway and stayed overnight at Skyland on the Skyline Drive. She loved the mountains, as I did. She always had. We walked and talked extensively. Her mind was keen, her body nimble, her energy still apparent. She was relaxed and enjoying every minute. I was too. It was a great visit.

My relationship with Elaine deepened. That old saying comes to mind — "Love is friendship caught fire." On September 20 Elaine and I were united by Peter, my former Episcopalian rector in a simple ceremony held in the beautiful and historic Lee chapel on the campus of Washington and Lee University. Only members of our immediate families were present, including our mothers and my new granddaughter, Jennifer. It was the perfect setting and we glowed with happiness. My older brother, Warner, was my best man. His wife, Betty, was Elaine's maid of honor.

The stirring marble memorial depicting the recumbent Robert E. Lee was just steps away as we made our solemn vows. The lovely lady who played the organ for the service stressed that the statue reflected Lee resting on the battlefield, not in death. We didn't question her explanation, but the reposing general was screened off by a sliding door and flowers for the ceremony.

We drove off from the luncheon reception to the historic Hotel Roanoke to spend a mini-honeymoon before returning to our respective jobs. I couldn't help but think of the vivid contrast between the simple spiritual ceremony showcased in that beautiful chapel and the elaborate, showy, and expensive one I had experienced in Greenwich. It was more meaningful.

I became increasingly pessimistic about the future of the radio station without some upgrading. Full-time operations seemed increasingly necessary if we wanted to compete successfully. Wally's two old-time employees continued to resent me and the management changes that affected them.

I noticed an ad in *Broadcasting,* the national trade journal, for a general sales manager at two radio stations in the Charlottesville, Virginia, market. With nothing to lose, I responded and talked with John, a young multi-business entrepreneur based in New York City. He had just bought an AM and an FM station there.

We arranged to meet in Charlottesville. I liked what I saw and heard in that meeting. John, in his early forties, was personable, open, and direct. He outlined his plans in detail, and I was impressed by them. I briefed him fully on my overall background and provided references. The genial meeting increased my interest. It was a major market, the home of Jefferson and the University of Virginia. It would add a new dimension to my radio experience. There was more competition, but I would be armed with two stations and full-time service. Both the challenge and the risk tempted me.

I sensed that John was just getting his feet wet in broadcasting and I felt that I had a good shot at the opening. I liked him from the outset.

"Look, why don't you think about this for a week or so," he said. "I have a plane to catch, but I will be back down probably the latter part of next week. I'll contact you then." We shook hands. I arrived home, and explained my continuing interest to Elaine. She was both understanding and supportive.

"I love Charlottesville. The job sounds great, but what about my shop here?" she asked.

"If by chance I get the job, I'll commute — it's about an hour. I can handle that and it will give us time to put everything in focus. It's no done deal yet."

The call from John came about a week later as promised, and he outlined an attractive, firm offer.

"Thanks, John, for the offer," I said. "I want to discuss it with my wife naturally and will get back to you tomorrow."

He stressed that he needed me as soon as possible. I figured that. Underneath, I felt the opportunity was not only excellent but advisable. Elaine was totally in agreement. "Go for it," she said.

I brooded over breaking the news to Wally, but sat down and composed my letter of resignation.

It is with sincere personal regret that I leave to accept a challenging position in Charlottesville. My decision was based purely on business considerations and the future . . . Working with a daytime-only station here precludes a promising future. . . . the selfish and resentful attitude of two entrenched key employees only hampers our effort. . . . The overall media competition is increasing . . . and I even urge you to seriously consider selling the station unless you are willing to invest in more equipment and seek a full-time frequency for the station, or preferably a full-time FM frequency for a new station, Wally. You can't live on the sentimentality of the past. You have cold hard business decisions to make.

My resignation hit him hard, but we salvaged our friendship with our usual openness. I called John and accepted his offer at a meeting that evening in Charlottesville. A few days later Wally and I arranged a final settlement including his buy-back of my recent limited stock investment. I gave him thirty days' notice. Fatherly Southern gentleman that he was, he gave me a bear hug, expressed his disappointment, and wished me success. "You'll do well." I appreciated his reaction and guessed then and there he would seriously consider the sale of his station.

It was a hectic time, and I needed a lift. One day I received a letter from the headmaster of St. Johnsbury Academy. He enclosed a newspaper article stating that St. Johnsbury Academy's Industrial Electricity-Electronics program had been cited by the U.S. Department of Education for having New England's Outstanding Vocational Education Program. Twenty regional awards were made nationally, but only three below the college or technical-school level.

The headmaster's letter read "I am sending this to you because you, more than anybody else, were responsible for the building of the vocational school and the merger of the old St. Johnsbury Trade School and St. Johnsbury Academy. I think you can be proud of what has happened in that effort. I know the move was controversial and difficult in the beginning, but I think the ugly duckling has turned into a swan. I am grateful to you for your foresight and your perseverance in the face of stiff opposition." It was a long, tough sell for the local school board.

His generous letter gave me warm satisfaction — the lift I needed. Finally, the effort by so many had paid off. The real credit rests with the dedicated and talented staff of the St. Johnsbury Vocational Center under the visionary leadership and administration of St. Johnsbury Academy.

I began my daily commute over the Blue Ridge Mountains to Charlottesville. Somehow the spectacular daily view from Afton Mountain on the crest stimulated me for the day's work ahead. I narrowed my efforts to sales and promotion for an AM country station and its full-time FM counterpart, Lite 102-FM, a soft-rock entry in the competitive Charlottesville media mix. I found an experienced salesman, Tommy, in place, and quickly added a sharp and energetic young woman, Lisa, to help blend our sales team. Lite 102-FM soon became a major factor in the broadcast scene although its coverage area was more limited than some of our competitors.

Soon Elaine and I agreed to rent a three-story town house in a convenient complex near the University of Virginia. We made the move. Elaine did a reverse commute back to her shop for a number of months until it was sold with a single classified ad placed in the *Washington Post*. Shortly after, at John's urging, we added Elaine to the staff and she found a natural niche in broadcast sales. We moved in to new sales offices on the downtown mall in the heart of the city.

We enjoyed our busier life in Charlottesville, and Troy joined us for a period before eventually heading for a Mennonite junior college in Indiana. We played tennis and swam at a local club. Troy starred on its local swim team in the summer and banged around in a red jalopy. Elaine and I usually attended "Fridays after Five" throughout the summer on the downtown mall. Huge crowds attended these mostly rock concerts sponsored by our stations and another business. My older daughter, her husband, my new grandchild, and Elaine's sons often visited our home with its great view of the mountains — and the swimming pool.

A delayed five-day honeymoon in Bermuda pumped more sunshine into the marriage. Acting on a reliable tip we stayed at the reasonable Stonington Beach Hotel. They had a tie-in with the College of Bermuda to train students in all aspects of hotel work and management. The staff was exceptional. They go overboard for honeymooners.

The soft sand beach, the crystal blue waters, and momentary rain showers provided an enchanting daily scene. We passed up joining the fast motorbike crowd to tour on foot and on a bus. We skirted the island shore in a small glass-bottomed, sight-seeing boat. We visited quaint shops, explored historic churches, and stopped at scenic points.

We flew back to the mainland, reluctantly leaving the romantic and friendly island. Bermuda had both educated us and brought our feelings for each other to a new high. It was a welcome brief retreat from our busy work world.

Back home I received a court-ordered citation from Vermont. My former wife wanted reimbursement for dental bills, support hosiery, and a prescription. I was not required to appear in court. My attorney represented me. The court ruling awarded her payment for the prescription prescribed for arthritic pain in her legs and held me liable for future prescriptions since her medical insurance didn't include prescription coverage. I was not held responsible for her dental bills and support hosiery under the divorce decree.

I learned that my youngest daughter had left her job, returned home to her mother's, and was taking courses toward a masters degree in Burlington. She was also working part time locally. I learned that a love interest had now entered her life.

In July 1983 Elaine and I traveled to my old Vermont hometown for Cindy's wedding to Stanley, a tall strapping policeman. The night before there was a dinner for the immediate families and attendants in a small, nearby country hall. It was my first meeting with the local family of the son-in-law to be, a somewhat awkward evening for us among strangers who pretty much ignored us.

The next morning Elaine got a good look at the interior of the home I had loved. The phone rang in our motel. It was a surprise call from my ex-wife.

"Cindy's hair needs some real attention. Do you think Elaine could come up and help with it?" she asked.

Naturally Elaine was glad to be of help but limited without her styling tools. Cindy looked radiant when she strolled down the long North Church aisle on my arm. The church was crowded, the service nice. At my suggestion, the reception that followed took place in the spacious and attractive dining area at the nearby college.

Again the situation was a bit awkward. It was the first time many of my old friends had seen me since I left Vermont, and there was an obvious inspection of my new wife. I couldn't hear any of the gossip but could imagine some. She was sixteen years younger than me and particularly stunning that day. The bride and groom left in a cloud of confetti, and we started the long way home.

We settled into hard work and a busy life in Charlottesville. Maybe we were too busy and under pressure. Maybe the age differential made a difference? Maybe my blood pressure medication was creating a problem? No. There was a counseling session but things settled down. Finally we started looking for a new home. We found it difficult in the immediate area of high-priced Charlottesville.

In time, I sensed that John was considering, or soon would, the sale of the stations. Based in New York, he was heavily involved in other business activities. I also sensed at my age I would be vulnerable in a change of ownership.

Elaine and I bought an attractive ranch house an hour over the Blue Ridge in Lexington. We made the move in August 1985 and commuted for a number of months. I resigned and handpicked my successor for John — an experienced woman from another station. I departed on excellent terms with mixed emotions. I was convinced he would end up selling the stations sooner rather than later, retrieving the investment and more.

I had already accepted a position as general manager for Lexington's two radio stations. They were owned by two brothers; one was a Washington attorney, the other worked at the stations in sales and commuted some distance. It was a logical step, sweetened by our new home there.

Our property was four miles from town in a rolling country setting that faced a striking panorama of the Blue Ridge Mountains to the east. A large screened-in porch adorned the front of the one-story red-brick ranch. The interior was made cozy and comfortable with our furniture. Built-in bookshelves and a colonial fireplace graced our living room.

The one-and-a-half-acre site included a large lawn shaded by towering mature maple and oak trees. The dogwoods, plum trees, and the old Jonathan apple tree created a spring maze of color. The site was all one could want. Nature was at its best.

Some painting and wallpapering came first. A new hardwood floor gave a rich look to the pine-paneled dining room. A slate patio enhanced a portion of the backyard, which was enclosed by a solid redwood fence. We had a three-room cinder block outbuilding for storage and a small insulated well house, the source of abundant water.

Elaine's dream of a fish pond with waterfall came true.

We added an access door to one end of the house, and Elaine's Hairstyling was reborn in an attractive room with new equipment and furnishings. Our green thumbs went to work all over the property adding color with shrubs, flowers, and a redbud tree. A large vegetable garden provided good, healthy yields. Live annual Christmas trees were given a permanent home. Birdhouses and feeders drew a variety of feathered friends.

We raked, mowed, and shoveled together. It was all a joint venture and we lavished work on our dreamland. I built and erected a picket fence and Elaine raised the fish pond population to twenty-three. We were happy in our new home.

We were active. We played some tennis in season, and attended football and basketball games at Washington and Lee. We went to church, enjoyed some social life on campus and in the community, and hosted an annual Christmas party for neighbors and friends in our festive home.

There were quarrels between the two owner-brothers at the local radio station that didn't bode well when the attorney's son joined the staff in an accounting role that further strained their relationship. I didn't mind the addition and continued to concentrate on the main mission of more revenues and better public relations. I had high respect for the absentee Washington attorney-owner and shared his goals.

I urged a local organization, Downtown Lexington, to inaugurate a series of local outdoor concerts in the summer months patterned on the successful venture in Charlottesville. We picked a sloping lawn area a few blocks from the center of the city owned by the university. "Fridays Alive" was born and continues to this day under a similar name. For the first time ever I saw Lexington's black and white communities commingling in public and obviously enjoying it. There was a slight rumble at the outset when beer was added to the list of refreshments available, but no problems developed after city council approval.

In March 1986 Elaine walked into the living room with an unexpected gift in a handheld wire carrier.

"Happy birthday," she exclaimed.

She smiled and presented me with a five-week-old, buff female cocker spaniel I named Corka.

"Just a minute," she said and returned to the car. She came in again holding a similar carrier.

"This one is mine," she said with a smile. "They're sisters. Mine is the runt in a litter of nine. They're registered purebreds. Their mother was black and white, Michael's Own Hannah. The father was buff, Artru Supersonic, a prize show dog champion."

"I don't believe this," I said with a corresponding smile. "They're so cute. This is great." I gave her a big hug as the little ones eyed their new home.

The next day with Elaine's carpentry skills coming into play we fashioned a large wired cage off the kitchen to contain the frisky pair.

Corka and Jenna did everything together side by side. They were inseparable, cute pups, and truly stunning as they grew. In time they mastered the "doggie door" that gave them access to the fenced backyard run. They loved their leash walks on the property. Like both of us, they were entranced by a bevy of quail that often waddled across our lawn, the squirrels, and occasional deer that happened by. We were now a family of four.

Corka and Jenna made a special hit when other members of our family visited, especially at Christmas. Jenna, the runt, was slightly smaller and more passive. Corka was more active. Both looked alike, but a blue collar on Jenna and a red one on Corka helped to identify them. They loved

Jenna and Corka

to ride in the station wagons and take long walks with us on the college campus.

I was thankful for the warm relationships I had forged with Elaine's three outstanding sons, particularly Troy, whom I knew better. It was an adjustment for all. Now seventeen, Troy wrote a note to his mother and me:

"Dear Mom and Dean: I know sometimes it might not seem like it, but I really am grateful for what you've done for me. . . . You are a very special part of my life that I wouldn't trade for anything. Once again I say thanks for just being there when I needed you. I *love* you." We were both heartened by his words. He was a real son to me.

Mother Finney had left an independent retirement center highrise in nearby Stamford where she had spent two years following the sale of her home. She had also had a hip operation, ended her driving years, and donated her beloved Buick to the garage attendant who had a need. Under the guidance of my older brother she moved to a fine independent retirement complex with extended health care facilities.

Elaine and I visited her on occasion, enjoying lunch or dinner with her. She was happiest when she had visitors. She seemed reasonably content, mixed with others some, but preferred the privacy of her room with a book and her television set. She still had her Bible near and her faith was intact. On several occasions her free spirit took over and she tried to bolt out the front door in her speeding wheelchair to fresh air and greener pastures. Someone prescribed medication to quell any further attempts. Her mental faculties were still remarkably good. I think she just wanted — out.

We often called my mother but soon noticed that our conversations with her on weekends evoked only slow unclear responses. This threw up a red flag. I wondered about medication and called the center, reaching a night supervisor who volunteered that she had been sedated on recommendation of the staff psychiatrist. Under my pressure steps were taken to cut the dosage and then to eliminate it. I wondered if the center was using a drug as a patient sitter in lieu of sufficient weekend staff.

On the home front Elaine provided a temporary scare when she entered the hospital for a biopsy on a suspicious lump in her throat. Todd, her middle son, and I were greatly relieved to learn that it was benign.

I find things often come in bunches. One night, after working late at the radio station, I fell off a darkened platform at the rear of the building. Dazed, I recovered and drove the four miles home. Elaine met me at the door.

"What on God's earth has happened to you? You have blood all over you!" she exclaimed. It was running down my face.

I quickly told her and she drove me to the emergency room at the local hospital. I was released after X rays and stitches below an eye and on my forehead. My glasses were broken.

I returned in a week to have the stitches removed and complained of pain. A new doctor had me X-rayed again and startled me with her report.

"You were right. You do have a problem — with a triple break to your cheekbone under your right eye. It will require immediate surgery," she said. "We'll notify your surgeon and make the necessary arrangements."

I entered the hospital the following day. The surgery had an unusual and unexplained result. A follow-up eye examination reflected no further need for glasses except for reading. I had worn bifocal glasses most of my life. My eyes were now several notches above 20/20. The longtime astigmatism in my right eye had completely disappeared. The ophthalmologist had no logical explanation. I was elated.

Maybe the incident was an omen — a good time to set my eyes on the future with a clearer vision?

t e n

The Way Out

Action and reaction, ebb and flow, trial and error —
change. This is the rhythm of living. Out of our over-
confidence, fear; out of fear, clearer vision, fresh hope.
And out of hope — progress.

BRUCE BARTON

Our cocker spaniels were loving family companions and enlivened our home. They were happy, bright, responsive, friendly, steady, and loyal.

One afternoon, Corka, a little more aggressive, pounced on a wet Brillo pad dropped on the kitchen floor. Down it went. We panicked. I guess Corka sensed the mistake. Up came the pad, soap suds and all. No problem.

One summer day I arrived home from work and opened the redwood gate to enter our fenced-in backyard. Corka and Jenna had access to it through their doggie door. There, stretched out along the house foundation, was a monstrous eight-foot, black, bloated snake with his head close to the doggie door. I retreated quickly to a side entrance to check the pups and alert my wife.

We peppered the snake with stones and he grudgingly slithered away to safety without a puppy cocker spaniel dinner. It was another introduction to country living. My neighbor, a former forestry agent, identified our uninvited guest as "just a big, old blacksnake on the prowl . . . your good friend in nature." He may have been, but we had reason to suspect his motive. We never saw our "friend" again and that was fine with us.

One day I received another contempt citation that stated that I had failed to reimburse certain expenses under the divorce decree. It was accompanied by a court-ordered summons requiring my appearance.

This time a personal court appearance in Vermont was inevitable. I contacted a new, highly recommended attorney in Vermont to represent me in the matter. He accepted, concluding that I had a good case. He filed a response to the court denying contempt and any money owed. He entered an affirmative defense claiming the bills were not "medical or hospital expense . . . within the contemplation of the court at the time of the divorce" in 1980.

The case went to superior court in April 1988 in my former Vermont hometown. My wife accompanied me, but naturally not to the courtroom. I had a lengthy meeting with my attorney the day before. My wife had seen the letters and knew of the phone calls from my ex-wife demanding reimbursement. She naturally had concerns.

I was accused of refusing to pay $19,241.61 for caretaking and housekeeping expenses billed to me as "nurses aides," social security taxes, accounting fees, some IRS payments including a late filing fee, and other items. I felt I was not responsible for such expenses under the original divorce decree.

My attorney took issue with my ex-wife's proposed interrogatories "addressed to the question of discovery of the assets of the Plaintiff, which is not relevant to the subject matter involved in the pending Motion."

I felt reasonably confident on the eve of the ordeal.

Court was held in a small informal room with a presiding judge and two local side judges present. My ex-wife appeared in a wheelchair. The atmosphere was somewhat relaxed.

In fairness, my former wife had undergone knee surgery in 1982 and used a walker, then crutches, and finally a cane to walk "until she no longer needed assistance to move about." In sympathy I absorbed "nurses aides" expenses influenced by the title, but had reason to believe the services were not what the name implied.

In 1986 there was a further weakening of her knee and late in the year she suffered a stress fracture of her tibia. She was hospitalized for eight days. Expenses for caretaking were again billed to me, in similar procedure, for reimbursement over and above medical expenses and insurance premiums for the period 1986 through March 1988 — a sum that had grown to a total of just over twenty-two thousand dollars. This time I had reason to refuse.

Tacy's attorney told the court that she had recently undergone a total replacement of her left knee and would face a similar procedure on the other knee.

At one point before the trial my attorney told me that my ex-wife's counsel suggested a settlement at a fifty-fifty split. I sensed a weakening in their case. After conferring with my attorney, I refused. The bills in question didn't fall within my responsibility under the terms of the original divorce decree that already was heavily weighted in her favor.

I left the courtroom that afternoon feeling calm and confident. I was relieved that it was all behind me. It didn't call for a victory celebration or vindictiveness on my part. In a way it was a sad day. I thanked my attorney for his efforts, and my wife and I returned to Virginia.

Weeks later I received the court's conclusions. The verdict specified the "motion for contempt and arrears is

DENIED." I actually received credit for an additional amount. Tacy also had to pay her attorney's fees. However, I believe if there had been proper interpretation of the rule of law in the first place it all could have been avoided. Oh well, the past is the past.

Then, after more than a year at the local radio stations I found myself again in the middle of a continuing feud between one owner and the other owner, who was his brother. I decided it was a no-win situation. Despite overtures I soon resigned and immediately took a sales executive position with two major stations in Roanoke, an hour's commute away. I was over sixty-five, but still fired up — willing and anxious to keep on working. Elaine's business was growing.

In early 1990 Elaine and I joined family members on the eve of the wedding of Judy, my older brother's lovely daughter. At forty-one, Judy was marrying for the second time. She had raised her equally lovely daughter, Laura, who was at her side. The future home of the couple was alive with laughter and obvious happiness.

Judy was radiant and bubbling. Her smile was contagious. The room crackled with conversation. Her husband-to-be, a practicing psychiatrist, circulated among the guests. He appeared calm, easygoing, but a little aloof. There was a strange twist in that his former wife was there with his family members. All in all it was a fun gathering.

After the buffet dinner I was sitting on a comfortable couch. Judy was sitting on the floor between my legs, her arms resting on my knees. She seemed buoyant and content. She rose to check something in the kitchen, walked across the living room, and suddenly dropped to the floor. There was an effort to revive her, but her life was over before a 911 call drew a delayed ambulance response. The scene was one of disbelief. Everyone was crushed by the turn of events. It was real — but unreal.

My older brother and his wife lost their only child that evening — bright and full of life one minute and gone the next. It reminded me how tenuous our hold on life is and accented the personal need for abiding faith. The occasion that night was one of the heart and it was ended by an unknown heart condition.

My work as an account executive for two major radio stations in the Roanoke greater market was a rewarding and challenging experience. I was a senior on the staff to say the least, but my young professional associates made me feel at home. I gained great respect for the ownership, management, and the professionalism of its overall staff. On the FM side, its Q99 had coverage in three states with 500,000 watts of power. The programming was a catchy blend of popular oldies and current hits — no hard rock. Its AM counterpart featured a variety of country music and the football and basketball schedules of nearby Virginia Tech.

My years there provided a logical ending to a broadcast career that had spanned fifty years. The daily commute and long hours were creating a strain on the marriage. I sought to correct that.

There were intervening trips to visit family members including my mother, now requiring extended care in a health facility. I vividly remember the last time I saw my mother at almost ninety-nine. Her frail body reflected her desire to go to her Maker. Elaine was in the room with me.

I leaned down and planted a kiss on my mother's forehead.

"I love you, Mom," was all I said.

Her eyes then opened ever so slightly. The trace of a smile crossed her face and her right arm slowly went up.

The fragile hand touched her lips and blew me that unforgettable kiss. I knew the end was near. Her long road, paved with faith, led upward.

There was a memorial service in the chapel of her beloved church in Greenwich. My two brothers added brief and eloquent remarks to those of her minister. Mine were contained as I flipped through the years in my mind. She was a remarkable human being, a tower of inner strength, and for me an ever-guiding light and inspiration. She was my loving mother — and substitute father.

In the chapel I looked around and realized that nowadays it takes a wedding or a funeral to bring all family members together. It seems scattered new roots hamper a collective presence at other times.

Mother began every day with faith, courage, and expectancy. For much of her lifetime she rose each morning with these simple words passed to her by Elizabeth, a dear friend:

> *Each morn when I awake, I say*
> *I place my hand in God's today.*
> *I know he will walk close by my side*
> *My ever-wandering feet to guide.*
> *When, at day's end, I seek my rest*
> *And realize how much I'm blessed,*
> *My thanks pour out to Him, and then*
> *I place my hand in God's again.*

Likewise her day always ended with an open Bible and a prayer. After losing her husband so early in life, Mother always looked ahead and never faltered. The past was the past. Her faith sustained her. She thrived on it and expected to be blessed each day. I believe she was. She took "love thy neighbor" to heart — those she knew and many she didn't. She expected the best, and I don't think living life disappointed her.

My mother's death in 1991, when she was nearly ninety-nine, naturally didn't come as any great shock. Nonetheless, I mourned her passing deeply and often revisited her life. I also mourned the fact I'd hardly known my father. I came to realize how much their love and lives had affected mine — and my brothers.

After my mother's death I soon discovered that she had saved every letter I had ever written her — from age seven at camp through college, war, and marriage. I also found several bulging scrapbooks and photo albums. They recounted my life in detail, much of which I had forgotten.

When my mother died I automatically reflected on those particular characteristics I admired in her and the degree to which she had passed some on to me. Faith, love, and caring were prominent. She was a private person. If she was down you didn't know it. She was always on the move. She was a terrific mother and grandmother.

She was always geared ahead. She was basically conservative, a little stubborn now and then, occasionally outspoken, but fair-minded.

In the fall of 1991 Elaine and I went to Greenwich for my fiftieth class reunion at Brunswick School. It was a return to the past for five of the original thirteen graduates as we toured the buildings and athletic grounds of a much larger school. We and our wives rooted for the football teams, attended some parties, and chewed over the old days. One returning classmate and friend was Rushton, a brother of Ethel Kennedy. We all enjoyed the late afternoon hospitality of the Skakels at their imposing Belle Haven home.

Elaine's mother was now living in Oregon. We knew why she had moved. Florence had an occasional phobia about items missing from her home and took extra precautions to bar her door. I found out that in the past she had blamed Elaine's ex-husband. We had problems with her in Virginia when she developed similar false thoughts about Troy. We attributed her accusations to misplaced items and just plain forgetfulness. However, our concern grew.

She was totally normal in all other respects. We discussed the matter with her young attorney, a good friend and trusted adviser. With his help we convinced Florence to seek help for the disturbing condition and she agreed. We took her to a highly recommended institution in Pennsylvania for an evaluation. We were thankful for her cooperation and hoped for the best.

She went through a week of examinations and then adamantly rejected any further treatment. She summoned us to "get me out." Elaine was told any reports were privileged information and would be sent only to Florence's attorney. The information never was shared, as far as I know.

Florence moved back to Oregon a few weeks later, urged on by a sister and her husband. We learned that they had warned her that if she stayed in Virginia she would be institutionalized. There was some suspicion on my wife's part that they hoped to gain some financial gain in this arrangement with Florence. I don't know.

Later on we traveled to Oregon to visit with Florence at her nice, small apartment. She was thrilled to see us and everything seemed normal. She turned happy tour guide for the capital city and the captivating Oregon coastline. We went to church with her, took her to her doctor, and met a few of her friends. Dinner with the sister and her husband was somewhat restrained. I sensed our presence was not a cause for rejoicing.

Months later Elaine returned to Oregon to be with her mother while she underwent surgery for cancer. Florence could not tolerate the chemotherapy treatments initiated afterward. She refused to continue and elected to maintain her quality of life until the end. We weren't surprised by her decision. Her deep faith spoke to that.

She had survived a poor and struggling childhood, leaving home at an early age to find work. I suspect she had experienced some mistreatment. Her original roots were fragile. She had a quirk or two — I think most of us do.

Maybe it was intuition, but upon Elaine's return home I grew concerned about her association with a good friend, our next-door neighbor. He had recently separated from his wife after a long history of major marital problems and had taken an apartment in an adjacent community. I couldn't understand the free haircuts — frequent for one almost bald. With some lingering doubt, I shrugged my suspicion aside. He was a close and trusted friend.

One night, weeks later, I came home from a local meeting. I remember Elaine had asked if I would be late. My wife wasn't home. There was a note saying she had left and would call me. Some clothes and household items were missing. The next morning I found her at my neighbor's apartment and learned that he had helped to move her things. I was stunned. I knew he had difficulties, but couldn't imagine he wanted more.

The next day Elaine called and said she was filing for divorce. I told her I would have to respond and would specify the situation and the person. We finally met for a lengthy discussion and reason prevailed. She returned home and wanted to work things out. I agreed. On November 22, 1993, the court issued an order of dismissal indicating "all matters between the parties have been resolved." I thought a mutually honest effort was underway, although I wasn't totally convinced.

It was a difficult time for us, but new hope and effort surfaced to help repair the damage. Fresh air blew into the marriage and caring was mutually expressed.

One morning I dropped in at a favorite local restaurant for a cup of coffee. It was often a hangout for golfers before they teed off at the local course. There he was — my former neighbor — and he couldn't avoid me if he wanted to. He walked over to me and spoke in a low faltering voice.

"Look, it just happened. I'm sorry. I'm really sorry. She's all mixed up," he said.

He started to go on and I stopped him. I was ticked off.

"You were a good neighbor and a great friend," I said. "You're the one that's all mixed up."

The words just came out. I was more sad than mad and still agonizing over what had happened.

"You aren't that good neighbor and friend anymore. Bug out," I said.

His face was flushed with a sheepish look. I think I even detected a few tears. He turned and left. I am sure he shot well over par on the golf course if he played. I left for home feeling under par. I didn't share the encounter with my wife.

A few weeks passed before Elaine's things were returned to our home. She made no effort to go for them at his place. Instead she instructed him to leave everything on a corner of our property and we retrieved them. It was an awkward situation.

I hoped that the entire affair was over and that we could pick up the pieces. We both loved our home and made the effort to do just that. Weeks later the former neighbor became our neighbor again, opting to return to his lovely home and troubled wife.

Florence visited us for Christmas. Her deep faith and spirit were still with her. She had a warm family get-together with her daughter and three grandsons, and was remarkably at ease.

One afternoon she was reading the local paper and her quiet self-composure evaporated. She was disturbed. There was a front-page story about a gift Pat Robertson and his wife gave to Washington and Lee — several hundred thousand dollars.

"Do you mean that he gave all that money to your wealthy college?"

"Yes, he was a former resident and college student here," I said. "His father was a United States senator who lived here."

"I will never send him another contribution," she announced. "He doesn't need it if he can do that."

I'm sure she regularly gave small donations to Robertson's religious organization and probably to Jerry Falwell's and John Hagee's, all cut from the ultraconservative cloth. She listened to them all on television.

I didn't want to add fuel to the fire, but I did venture a comment.

"I just feel he is divisive, mixes politics and religion too much. I have more regard for the words and efforts of Billy Graham or Robert Schuller than a Pat Robertson or Jerry Falwell."

I thought to myself how such preachers preyed on the well-intentioned elderly like Florence: alone at home, sending money they cannot afford to fund the high cost of television.

In January, Elaine received word that her mother had less than a month to live. She made arrangements to fly out immediately. One day before leaving Elaine asked me to make a bank deposit for her shop. I went to get the zippered bag and opened it. By pure chance I found it also contained some letters with the return address of a doctor in a nearby town. I was both curious and concerned, so I opened them.

The letters were of a personal nature, not medical, some written on personal stationery. One contained a lengthy analysis of Elaine's handwriting, which was highly commendatory and emotional. Under the circumstances I decided to have them copied, and then returned them to the bag. I said nothing as Elaine readied for her flight to Oregon.

Soon after I sent a three-line note to the doctor telling him not to contact my wife. I'm sure he was surprised. One letter to Elaine stated:

> Don't feel you must hold on to anything I send you. Remember the essence of anything I write and then trash the evidence unless you have near certain ways to avoid discovery. . . . I am enjoying learning about the Sagittarius woman . . . one of the books I bought says that firstborns or only's make the best matches for last-borns.

A doctor? I wondered what kind. I did learn she had only recently met him through a friend, a nurse at a mental hospital.

Needless to say I was upset. I decided to terminate my commute. I resigned and turned my attention to some free-lance marketing and public relations work for the growing Virginia Horse Center, one of the finest equestrian centers in the country, which was just a half-mile from our home. My efforts helped to reestablish the Rockbridge County Fair at the center after a fifty-year hiatus.

As early as 1828 there had been agricultural fairs in the county. At the outbreak of the Civil War the Confederacy rented the fairground and buildings to enlist troops and use as a hospital.

I remembered being hustled off to the fair in September 1941 as a college freshman rushed by fraternity upperclassmen. Admission was twenty-five cents and one lucky person purchased a Ford for one dollar. The thrill at the fair was the Silver Streak ride. One questionable surprise caught a lot of eyes — a man and a slinky woman behind a see-through curtain performed an act usually done in privacy. War terminated the county fair when bombs fell on Pearl

Harbor. Bigger and better, it was back — no see-through curtain.

The news from Oregon was unchanged. Florence was hanging on with Elaine's good care. At home, Corka, my beloved cocker, contracted a virus that struck quickly and she passed away on Valentine's Day. Jenna, her smaller sister, and I moped around together. Her grief was obvious, and she stuck to me like glue. Corka had been special to us both.

Soon after I made several trips to Vermont to check on Aunt Petie. My brothers and I were her only remaining family. She had been ill, had suffered a fall, and life was closing in on her at ninety-nine. There was some concern about the reputation and reliability of her attending physician. Her druggist had led me to question her medication. When I made a surprise visit to her doctor to discuss my aunt's condition I received a cold reception. He was unimpressive and uncooperative. I left concerned.

Independent Petie did not welcome live-in help and daytime nursing service. She didn't take well to my having her washer and dryer replaced either. With a tart tongue she reminded me that she made the decisions. Of course the machines hadn't worked for years. Laundry had been sent out and returned a week later. Now that she was bedridden there was a real need and there was someone to do laundry. Things finally calmed down. She enjoyed her live-in helper *and* the fact that she was a good card player.

In April, Jenna and I drove to Vermont to look in again on Petie, who was now in a hospital. She was nearing the end. A few days later, by her own choice, she returned to her beautiful home to die. Petie was a strong-willed and occasionally wily woman who commanded attention, but she also had an enticing soft side that endeared her to others. She had ignited my love for wildflowers and was the harbinger of my meadows in Lexington.

At about the same time I received a letter from Florence. It both lifted and dropped my spirits. I questioned if she was aware of her daughter's decision to separate.

> I want to thank you for your love, your kindness to our family, and your warmheartedness and consideration for all of us. I am sure this is not always the case in second marriages. . . . and I want to say I appreciate it very much. God bless you and your goodness to all of us. . . .
>
> I am believing in God for his healing and I trust Him for his protection of Elaine coming out and while she is here . . . may our Loving Father keep you too as you are there. Sometimes God heals through channels of death and if he decides to do that it is okay. I am ready. Heaven is my ultimate goal. . . .
>
> And so I want you to know I love you and thank you for being so good to my precious daughter and to me. Maybe this sounds odd, but I think it is proper. Thank you for your prayers.

It was my last communication with Florence.

The surprise letter convinced me that she did not know about Elaine's affair with the doctor. I wished I knew more than I did about the family's early days, especially Elaine's. There was always a minor strain in Elaine's relationship with her mother. I couldn't put my finger on it. Maybe it was her mother's outward and rampant religious zeal. Maybe it was her strange behavior when she lost or misplaced personal possessions. I don't know.

Elaine's time with her mother far exceeded the estimated timetable. Weeks turned into months. Both had endured a similar experience caring for the father in his final days. I remember Florence as a caring, hardworking, and gifted woman who traveled from a disheartening start to her reward with uncompromising faith.

Florence's letter made me think about trying to save the marriage. Perhaps it was too late or not to be. I would just have to wait. For some reason I developed a fatalistic attitude of "whatever" — life goes on.

I had already turned increasingly to prayer and faith in my daily life. Each night my prayers concluded with words similar to this: Lord, be with me, stay with me, guide me, and take me where you will. I found reassuring peace and confidence in relying on Him as I entered an uncertain future once again.

Elaine returned and found an apartment in the nearby city where her doctor-friend was employed. She underwent extensive counseling on her return. I joined her in one highly emotional session. I requested a private follow-up meeting with the counselor, who said, "Let her go." I am sure that Elaine's earlier life, prior divorce, our separation, her mother's death, and other factors were involved. I also sensed that my age had become even more of a factor after her mother's difficult battle with cancer.

I sought a change with several trips to see my Vermont family, now increased by two fine granddaughters, Sara and Stacy. They live in a scenic country area near St. Johnsbury. On one occasion I delivered my beloved Old Town canoe to them, believing it would have a better life there. They have an inviting lake nearby. (I was shocked to learn there are only two natural lakes in all Virginia.)

eleven

Second Time Around

The theories of faith are many.
The certainties of faith are few.
The theories of faith are complex.
The certainties of faith are simple.
The theories of faith are incidental.
The certainties of faith are vital.

JOHN MCCLELLAN HOLMES

I found diversion from my marital troubles creating a wild-flower meadow and a series of smaller scenes at natural sites on the property. It became a major hobby. I reveled in the beauty created by the mix of perennials enhanced by borders of annuals. The wide variety provided ever-changing colors that lasted into November with only minor care.

I worked long and hard to prepare the meadow site by hand and to till it. It meant I would have to mow the former field area only once after the first frost. I spread seeds by hand. I flipped an four-by-eight-foot piece of plywood to stomp on them.

The meadow and natural niches offered a blaze of core-opsis, cornflowers, red poppy, and cosmos that blended with lupine, sweet William, black-eyed Susans, and daisies. More color came from the butterflies that moved in. Now and then a cottontail would dart out, and an occasional deer would stop by at dusk. Even a family of quail seemed happy with my colorful creation — as was I.

I owe my interest in wildflowers to the Boswell Botany Trail in Manchester, Vermont, and to mountain hikes and canoe portages of the past. The seeds all came from the Vermont Wildflower Farm in Charlotte. The dazzling scene often slowed and stopped passersby and tourists. It was unique. For me it was just that nature had once again stirred my imagination. It was good exercise and a peaceful pastime too.

However, divorce was on the docket. The phone rang and it was my attorney. He told me a letter was going to my wife's attorney that included the following:

> I believe you should be aware that my client has
> ample proof . . . on the part of Elaine. Given the
> fact this is only a thirteen year marriage, the second
> for each, I do not believe any court would grant her
> such a lump sum. . . . We do not have much time to
> resolve this without making the allegations in a
> cross-bill. . . . Let us know your client's position on
> this as soon as possible.

Elaine had already had a throat biopsy that had proved to be benign. A more serious scare was just ahead. In December, while she was walking in a mall, one leg went numb. She called her regular specialist who had been treating her for an arthritic condition. He told her to go to her local hospital emergency room at once. She needed surgery on her back. An old car accident injury was suspect.

My wife said her doctor directed her to a neurosurgeon in a small city some distance away. She made an appointment and went with her son Todd. A surgery date was set. I took issue with her course of action and strongly urged a second opinion. I questioned why the highly regarded University of Virginia Medical Center, just minutes away, had been bypassed by her doctor. I was naturally skeptical about the role of her new friend. He was a medical doctor employed by the state at a nearby institution.

I strongly urged her to consult our trusted family doctor for advice and she finally agreed. This led to an appointment with Dr. Edward Jane, a noted neurosurgeon with a national reputation at the University of Virginia Medical Center. He had performed the surgery on Christopher Reeves following his accident. Elaine canceled her prior arrangement.

Ten days later Elaine underwent six and a half hours of critical surgery for the fusion of four lower vertebrae in her back. Todd and I waited it out and were finally informed of its success. A short time later I went to her room and found her doctor-friend waiting for her return from recovery. It was not a pleasant encounter.

She was soon transferred to a motel for weeks of treatment at a nearby therapy center. Both had a hospital tie-in. I visited with her a number of times for lunch and provided transportation on occasion. The overall surgery costs were heavy, but I covered her expenses.

One night I returned home and reread a letter from my stepson Todd that had bolstered my spirits and also tore at them. It was a reflection on his upbringing and meant a great deal to me.

> I just wanted to send you a quick note to let you
> know how much I appreciate you, and to encourage
> you. This is long overdue . . . it must have been
> difficult to enter a new family with three young
> men such as Eric, Troy, and myself. . . . I want you

to know how much I appreciate what you've done
for Mom, and what you mean to her. You are very
special to her!

I wondered about that.

I also want to thank you for what you've meant to
me. . . . I appreciate your support, love, and for
always being there for encouragement and advice. . . .
    It occurs to me that you've had kind of a rough
couple of months recently . . . plenty to occupy your
mind. . . . It is testimony to your strength and
perseverance that you've maintained your great
outlook and attitude through moves and job
changes . . . your mother's failing health, Mom's
surgeries, Warner's tragedy, and the trials and quirks
of three wayfaring stepsons. Especially recently, I
guess Troy and I have provided a lot of entertaining
food for thought for Mom and you. . . .
    I really feel at home with you and Mom, and
appreciate the models you two have provided for
me. . . . Take care of yourself, and I hope to see you
and Mom before too long.

The reading helped, but left me wondering how I had
reached this point. Come what may, I determined to maintain my relationships with the three stepsons I had come to
love and respect.
    Elaine finally returned to her apartment. She added a
lively white miniature poodle as a companion. It was not a
timely decision in any way. The apartment management
unexpectedly notified tenants that dogs would no longer be
allowed to reside in the complex. Residents were notified
they had thirty days to rectify the situation. Her doctor-

friend came to the rescue, taking Gidget into his double-wide mobile home in an adjacent community.

Our divorce was quietly finalized with no court appearances. Elaine was extremely well treated under the circumstances. I was determined to retain the real estate. She took only limited furnishings in addition to her shop equipment. We were friendly.

I now had the home to myself with her cocker spaniel, Jenna. I was concerned about the doctor who had entered Elaine's life. I thought she should be too, but she moved in with him thirty days later and they were married there. I vowed to put it all behind me as I contemplated a confused future again.

I decided to get my home and property in mint condition and thought about selling. I cleared more land and added a grove of stately pine trees to screen an outbuilding. The lawns, field, and landscaping had never looked better. I put on a new roof and added a new furnace. I painted the attractive three-room storage shed inside and out. The fish pond was cleaned and its waterfall improved. The well was checked. The property was ready for sale. I wasn't sure I was, but alone at my age it made sense.

I thought of a return to Vermont, and the Manchester and the Middlebury–Lake Dunmore areas came to mind as possible destinations. I would be nearer to family members in Vermont and Connecticut, but I loved my present place in the Shenandoah Valley of Virginia. What to do?

On a Saturday in early July I received a phone call from the Saturn dealership in Roanoke advising me that the exact model and color I was looking for was now in their lot. On Monday I drove down and was met by Janet, an attractive sales representative. She didn't have to sell me on the station wagon. I knew exactly what I wanted.

"I'll take it," I said, after a short trial spin.

Saturn prices are firm — no haggling. I traded and indicated I would pay cash on the balance. I returned the next day to take possession in a showroom lined with staff members. The little ceremony over, Janet indicated she would give me a full rundown on operation of the Saturn and answer any questions I might have. We sat in the front seats to converse and quickly our talk took a different tack.

I was taken with her outgoing personality and obvious talent. She had a real spark and it lit on me. I figured she was in her late twenties and could really sell — not just cars.

"How long have you been selling Saturns?"

"Oh, about a year here and about the same at a dealership in North Carolina before I came back to this area," she said.

"You're from here then?" I said.

"Yes, we had a family-run marble and granite business. My dad and older brother were the key guys in an operation that included fabricating, finishing, and installation. We did all kinds of jobs — residential and commercial, even banks. They did beautiful work."

"Did you work there too?" I asked.

"I dropped out of college at one point to help," she said. "Dad had an accident that left him with a bad back. Then my brother was injured — a marble slab came down on his foot. Dad was key to figuring jobs and sales. My brother oversaw the installations. We had a number of employees."

"What did you do?" I asked.

"A little of everything — kept the books, tried to keep things going. We had to give up fabricating, and I arranged to have it done by a firm in Georgia and had it shipped in. It changed our operating procedures, raised our expenses, and made things really difficult all around."

"I can see that it would. How about your dad?" I said.

"Not good — in constant pain — can't do much."

"So what happened to the business?" I asked.

"We gave up after struggling for a year or so — had to close down. It was too much, but I loved the work. Dad's with my mother down in southwest Virginia. My brother lost a couple of toes. He started a small metal business and is doing okay."

"I gather then you left to work somewhere else?" I said.

"Yeah, I ended up selling Saturns in Carolina. Did okay. What do you do?"

"Well, I've been in broadcasting all my life in Vermont and Virginia. My last job was for two radio stations here. I've been doing some freelance marketing and public relations work lately. Going to take a little time off and head this new Saturn to Vermont next week," I said.

"Do you have family there — or in Lexington?"

"I have a daughter and family in Vermont. I lived there for more than thirty years. I have a daughter and family in Pennsylvania too. I have a home in Lexington — no family now except a prize cocker spaniel. I've just been through a tough divorce I didn't need, and I'm considering a move to southern Vermont — going up to look around," I said.

She said she had a roommate who shared her local apartment and that she had one sister in the area, another in the Midwest. She got out of the car.

"Thank you, sir. I appreciate your business and wish you the best on your trip. Any problems, give me a call. I'll probably be here when you come in for your first service." She extended her hand, long brown hair framing her smiling face.

It was certainly an interesting and unusual experience. I was impressed with Saturn's overall welcome and service, and particularly with the friendly and responsive sales representative. For some reason I felt that she was biding time, waiting for a better opportunity. I could understand.

I took off to comb southern Vermont for a new place to live and arrived in Manchester, that beautiful resort town on the edge of Bromley and Stratton ski areas where my aunt and uncle had lived.

I looked at condominiums and town houses, including several high on a hillside with a commanding view of the Green Mountains. Can't get away from them. I encountered some long lines of bumper-to-bumper traffic working their way toward Manchester's fabulous big-name shopping complexes and sensed the problem would be even greater when thousands of skiers came in winter months. Manchester was now overrun with well-healed transients and newcomers and I decided to explore elsewhere.

I left for Springfield, less than an hour away. I was drawn back to the Hartness House, the imposing stone mansion once owned by a former Vermont governor, my favorite country inn.

It inspires relaxation with its handsome wooden spiral, red-carpeted staircase, the white banisters and cherry hand-rail leading up to the period-furnished Charles Lindbergh room and others. You are drawn to a living room with a mammoth stone fireplace opposite an inviting, colorful, and romantic dining room with pink tablecloths, unique chandeliers, and picturesque windows. No wonder the inn is a mecca for weddings and special occasions. It's outstanding.

For the next few days I looked at town houses, condominiums, and apartment complexes around the area. I found a few I could consider. I wasn't interested in going farther north, where I knew the winters were worse and where I would be returning to memories that I wanted to forget.

The trip was helpful. I headed home for Virginia pretty well convinced that I would return to live life out in Vermont.

In the weeks that followed I was convinced that I should sell, find a place in southern Vermont, and take Jenna with me. The Vermont trip had helped to get me back on track. I was down. I guess I was a living example of that old saying "marry in haste, repent in leisure." Strangely I felt no animosity toward Elaine. I was sad and honestly concerned for her. I was embarrassed by it all too.

Weeks later I took my Saturn in for service and ran into Janet again. We talked just briefly. She said she had been asked to do some accent work in a new store showroom that included a marble fireplace, hearth, and countertops. She knew how to reenter the field and had the drive to back it up. I encouraged her.

Several weeks later I returned to Roanoke on other business and met Janet. We talked over coffee. She had completed her first marble installation and said that the job had led to two more offers. She took me to see the work and it was strikingly tasteful. The owners praised her. It was obvious that she knew what she wanted to do — to gradually build a full-time business.

I had all but decided to move back to Vermont, but I had some reservations about those cold hard Vermont winters. Janet's desires reminded me of my own small risky start in broadcasting at a similar age. We talked again and I volunteered to help her finance two pending jobs involving marble countertops.

I returned to Vermont to look for a new residence, to see my younger daughter again, and to make a hospital call on my first wife who had undergone a hip replacement. When I got home I learned that she had fallen during supervised walking therapy following the surgery. There was some question about the therapist's responsibility, but it was not pursued.

Complications led to several months in a rehabilitation center. I returned and brought Tacy's sister from Connecticut to visit her. She went to another care facility closer to her home. It was a long and costly period.

Back in Virginia I contacted Janet. She was obviously encouraged. After serious thought I postponed a return to Vermont. I offered to help her and to merge our restless talents and experience. The prospect of helping to establish a marble and granite interior accents business hit me. I was intrigued, excited, and hoped that I could also eventually gain a source of income.

Janet established an office on the dining-room table in her apartment. A computer was installed. JLC Stoneworks, Inc. was in the making. I learned from her and her ailing father. Soon I scoured the Shenandoah Valley to dig up leads from architects, contractors, kitchen-bathroom dealers, and interior decorators. My broadcast sales experience in the area helped. It was interesting work and I gave it my full effort. It was good therapy after difficult times.

My young partner covered the greater Roanoke area. I covered the area north. She followed up on our leads with cost estimates and necessary bids. She oversaw product selection, made fabrication arrangements, and supervised actual installations by independent contractors, including her brother, who helped us get started. We worked hard. I helped to arrange competitive fabrication sources in Virginia, Pennsylvania, and Vermont. We had to buck a big well-established corporate competitor with fabrication facilities in our general market area. Personal service was most important.

We reversed our decision to move our office to central Lexington in favor of Roanoke. In light of everything, I decided to sell my home and move to Roanoke and devote time to building the fledgling firm. I contacted a good friend who was a realtor and listed the property with her agency. I thought it would not sell until spring, but I was wrong. My home was sold in a few days.

I made a single Sunday afternoon trip to search for an apartment in the Roanoke area. Just by chance I found one in a nice private location on my very first look. It was exactly what I wanted, and my dog was welcome too. The mountain views helped. I later learned that my youngest daughter had lived in this same complex for a short time after college graduation. Small world. I was reminded of my older daughter's kidnapping when I passed a nearby intersection.

The closing on the house was accomplished in a reasonable time. I wondered if my dog would live to make the move with me, and she did. Her heart was failing, and she was on medication. Jenna made an unexpected and amazing rally and loved her new environment. She thrived on our daily walks along a lovely wooded lane that was almost at our door. She was leaner and younger. It was difficult with my busy schedule to properly attend to her, but it was my responsibility. She was family and my loving friend.

I found myself returning to Lexington regularly on business and for pleasure. I would drift back for the "Fridays Alive" concerts, which I helped to organize. Jenna came with me on many of my wanderings, and she loved Goshen Pass as much as I did. She was welcome company.

In a bold business move Janet and I bought an older house in an attractive residential area for office space and a private showroom. It also provided an upstairs apartment for Janet. Almost immediately we were harassed by a difficult neighbor. She had helped to uncover and expel someone engaged in drug activity in a nearby house. I guess the additional traffic aroused her suspicions. In a year we sold the house at a small profit and moved the office into the lower level of a town house occupied by Janet and a friend.

It was a hot humid day in August when I found Jenna hardly moving about. I rushed her to the animal clinic. She had been loved by the attentive staff there all of her life.

The next day I was told that she was not responding to

treatment. Jenna was very special to me, and it was a hard decision to put her to sleep. I went back to her cage to see her one last time. She was motionless and her eyes were closed. I leaned down, kissed and stroked her forehead. All of a sudden she lifted her little head and looked right at me.

"I love you, Jenna," I said.

Her head dropped. Tears dampened my eyes. Ed, the veterinarian, assured me she was in no pain.

I returned to the clinic the next day and met the veterinarian.

"Just after you left I had to take a phone call in my office," he said. "When I returned to take care of Jenna, it wasn't necessary. She had already passed on peacefully."

"I'm glad. Were you surprised?"

"No, I've seen it before. Dogs are loyal and loving to their loved ones right 'til the end. She was waiting for you so she could check out," he said.

His words got to me. My grief was heavy and lingered as I left. My little best friend, my companion to the end, was gone. I felt alone. I recalled the similar scene at my mother's bedside.

I know that cocker spaniels "talk." I presume all dogs do. Mine did — sometimes vocally with a quick bark, a rare whine, but more with body language and facial expressions, or a cute cocked head.

I can't think of a better investment in life for the cost and return these two cocker spaniels provided. Add good care, steady attention, and abiding love to a quality dog, and you get back an even temperament, true affection, natural beauty, fun, and steadfast loyalty to the end. They are a responsibility. They add to life. They are family.

twelve

Out of the Blue

Grow old along with me!
The best is yet to come.
The last of life for which
the first was made.

ROBERT BROWNING

My work took me on a number of trips to marble and granite fabrication plants outside the state, including one near Rutland, Vermont. I thought again of an eventual return to Vermont. I was surprised to learn that the first marble quarry in the nation was started in East Dorset in 1785, although I knew the granite quarries in the Barre area were among the largest and deepest in the world.

In mid-1997 I was troubled by uneasiness. I knew that our small business needed more effort, more help, and more dollars to compete and succeed in a wide area. It would also take time. It is one thing to launch an enterprise. It's another to build it up and sustain it in a competitive market. I was conscious of my age. My partner was young, talented, and hardworking. She was like an adopted daughter.

My thoughts again turned to Vermont. I decided to live out my years trying to be productive in a small town there. I thought of writing a book. I was also conscious of family ties and friends in Vermont and Connecticut. I paddled through Green Mountain lakes in my mind.

One day when passing through New Market I stopped to see my old friend Wally. He was confined to bed with round-the-clock care, but his mind was still keen. The former robust and talented athlete was down to just ninety-six pounds. He had heard about the breakup with Elaine and offered this advice:

"Just remember this too will pass. The sooner you know these things the better. Think of the future and to hell with the past. We have all had our problems," he said.

He went on. "May God hold you in the palm of his hand always, my friend. Take care and God bless. Just be yourself and I am sure everything will work out."

His voice dropped and I leaned over the bed to listen.

"Where there is song there is no evil. Where there is evil there is no song. We have all made mistakes you better believe. Go have a good drink and don't worry. . . . You are always welcome in my house," he said with a wavering voice and stretched-out hand.

The loud voice was no more. The big heart was still there. Wally was a unique individual from the "ole South." Our political thoughts were different — little else. He could be tough one minute, gentle the next. His language now and then could melt the snow. He revered his longtime black handyman and the feeling was reciprocated.

I left knowing I would not see him again. He was a complicated character, a caring person, a good man, and good friend. I recalled his warm and friendly visits with my family. He had been full of fun — the complete Southern gentleman.

In mid-December, by pure chance, I heard about a friend I had known years ago in Vermont. Surprisingly, the information came in a phone conversation with Tacy. Elsie attended the same church. Her older son and our older daughter had been classmates in high school. She had worked in the dental office our family went to.

I was surprised to learn that she had divorced her husband just before I left Vermont in 1979. I was even more surprised to learn that she had not remarried and was living in an apartment next to the church we all had attended. On the spur of the moment I sent her a Christmas card, adding a few casual lines.

I visited my older daughter and family for Christmas and continued on to Vermont to visit with my younger daughter, her husband, and my two grandchildren. On a Sunday afternoon I entered my old hometown, drove down the handsome main street, and remembered that Elsie lived next to the church.

I hadn't seen a soul, and then the unexpected happened. There she was walking in front of the house. I recognized her instantly as I passed. I went around the block and when I returned another woman had joined her for a walk. I went on and checked in to a motel.

Later I decided to call her. Instead I got in the car, went to her door, and took her by complete surprise. She invited me in to her attractive and neat third-floor apartment. We spent several hours catching each other up on our respective lives. I had known her for thirty years, not seen her in twenty.

Elsie was eight years younger. In the twenty years of separation the only change was that the attractive brunette had become a stunning senior with sparkling gray hair. The ready smile was still in place, and she was slim and trim. We traveled in different circles when I had lived there, but I had always noticed her good looks and cheerful way.

She had divorced for understandable reasons, had two sons in the area — a granddaughter and another grandchild on the way. She had recently retired as director of a small retirement and care facility for the elderly and was doing some part-time accounting work for a dental office.

We went out to lunch the next day. That evening I visited my daughter and her family. The next morning I went to a marble company enroute to Virginia. I wished there had been more time in Vermont. This new interest that had unexpectedly entered my life strengthened my resolve to return to Vermont.

Elsie and I kept in contact through letters and phone calls. On January 31 we met again in Vermont, a hundred miles removed from the hometown and local gossip. Four of the most memorable days of my life followed in the warm atmosphere of the Hartness House, that special country inn. We shared sight-seeing, good food, lengthy conversations, a movie, and brisk walks. I wanted our newfound relationship to flourish. We had so much in common. I hoped she shared my feelings. I felt that I had finally found my kind of woman.

Our relationship evolved quickly and naturally. We weren't strangers, we were old friends. We were open, had much in common, and continually found more. Numerous trips to Vermont followed and we decided to join our lives. Neither of us wanted to emulate the growing practice of living together without marriage.

I invited her to come to Virginia with me and to meet members of my family on the way. We spent several hours inspecting the college town of Middlebury as a possible future residence but left for Virginia a little disappointed. We arrived at my older daughter's home in Carlisle, Pennsylvania, to a warm family welcome that included my teenage granddaughter, Jennifer.

The next morning we continued the trip, entering the scenic Shenandoah Valley. The Blue Ridge Mountains drew comparisons with the Green Mountains we had left. We stopped in Lexington and I became a tour guide, showing

Elsie historic sites, the two colleges, and my previous home. She was impressed by the small city and the striking surrounding mountains.

Three days followed in Roanoke exploring and deepening our relationship. The selection of a diamond engagement ring cemented our decision. We soon decided that Lexington would be our home and planned to visit Vermont regularly.

We started the return trip and stopped for an enjoyable visit with my older brother and his wife in Connecticut. They received Elsie with genuine warmth and approval as I knew they would. A closeness developed then and there.

I made numerous trips back to Vermont to be with Elsie and to meet with her sons' families. I was with her at the hospital when her grandson, Gunnar, was born. I never thought I would return to my hometown, let alone be married there. I'm sure no one else did either. Eight hundred miles and twenty years separated us. It kindled some awkwardness with my younger daughter, who was reminded of my divorce there years before.

We were married in June 1998 in Elsie's church, my former one, with just a few family members present. The simple, moving service was filled with love and understanding. My best man was my close friend and attorney, John, the best man I had known there in thirty years. Elsie's maid of honor was her lovely young granddaughter, Erin, which added a special note.

The minister, Jay, spoke eloquently of commitment with words from Ruth that we had agreed on:

"Wherever you go, I shall go. Wherever you live, so shall I live. Your people will be my people, and your God shall be my God too. Wherever you die, I shall die, and there shall I be buried beside you. We will be together forever, and our love will be the gift of our life.

"That's the commitment you make to each other today. ... Elsie, like Dean did years ago, you'll be moving from the Green Mountains to the Blue Ridge Mountains . . . but when you lift your eyes to the hills it will be the same mountain range you're looking at. Those hills will always be a link between Vermont and Virginia, and a reminder of home, and, as often you have assured us, point the way back to us. . . .

"But more important, those hills are a reminder of where your help comes from. They point beyond themselves to their Maker. Your help comes from the Lord who made heaven and earth. These commitments, as great as they are, are made possible by this greatest of commitments: Your God shall be my God.

"Your relationship includes a third party who is the Author of this day. I speak of the Lord, our God, whose hand is at work helping to create this union. . . . Knowing God is with you can make all the difference. The togetherness you pledge will take you even unto the most exotic, most unknown realm — the realm beyond this life."

The young pastor's words were richly moving, and there was a loving expression by all at the conclusion of the modest service.

We left the church for an intimate family get-together, and then spent a few days at the place that had helped to bring us together, the Hartness House. We returned to pack and clear Elsie's apartment. The moving van with attached car carrier arrived from Virginia, was packed, and took off. We soon followed, our spirits high and our love meshed, headed for a new life in the Shenandoah Valley.

In the days and weeks ahead I often reflected on how unusual it was that our paths had crossed again after so many years. The meeting surely came "out of the blue" — with a guiding hand?

We married after only six months, but we had known each other in the past and quickly discovered the common interests in our current lives including family and church. I knew how highly her community, and especially her church, regarded Elsie. I got the word everywhere. I sometimes felt guilty that I was taking her away. When we met again after so many years, Elsie had just been designated a deacon emeritus by her church. A written tribute was sent to the congregation and included these words:

> Elsie's giving spirit is unflagging . . . unpretentious
> and undemanding . . . has been serving others all
> her life . . . over the past fifty years has been serving
> this church effectively in many ways — teacher,
> choir member, every committee of the church,
> treasurer of missions for thirty years.

The statement indicated that church figures, their attitudes and lifestyles, had influenced her in her formative years.

> Stewardship is Elsie's life — giving what is needed,
> where it is needed, and being sensitive to those
> changing needs, and expecting nothing in return.
> She is also attentive to the needs of her family.

I consider myself a lucky man and am determined to hold up my responsibility in the union.

Elaine heard of my pending marriage. She wrote:

> I must say it did hit me between the eyes. A part of
> me feels sad and another part of me says, hey wait a
> minute . . . look what I've done . . . want you to be
> happy . . . have had some wonderful experiences
> together . . . as I look back on all that has happened,

some of it could have been avoided, but then we can't cry over spilled milk, can we? As you said, life goes on. We now have other bridges to build. . . . I do wish you well. Best to you always.

I was appreciative.

My first wife's bitterness still smolders when she thinks of the past. Recently she told me that the mother of the young woman who entered my life had apologized for her daughter's actions, indicating she had been a very independent daughter. I said nothing in return, but felt if anyone should apologize I should — to her mother. I would tell her that she and her late husband could take great pride in their daughter. Our relationship was real and clean, not unseemly — well understood by some. Tacy and I have periodic contact in regard to our wonderful daughters. Our relationship is friendly, yet restrained. Some differences still exist.

The Bible says:

Love is patient, love is kind. It does not envy, it is not proud, it is not rude. It is not self-seeking, it is not easily angered, it keeps no record of wrongs. Love does not delight in evil, but rejoices in the truth. It always protects, always trusts, always hopes, always perseveres. Love never fails. (Corinthians 13:4–8a)

I speak with more experience than most! Love is caring, but mutual commitment is needed to keep a marriage healthy. I think a key factor in that commitment is to express your love and caring passionately in words, deeds, and actions every day. I'm positive Elsie and I are fully committed. Better late than never, and I am thankful to Him, and to her.

We are in the crowning years of retirement in the beautiful, historic two-college town of Lexington. We have more time to enjoy life, and our days and nights sing in complete harmony. We work together, play together, talk together, love together, and show respect for each other. Happiness pervades our bright, pleasing home and our activities. Now and then I plop on the comfy living-room couch in front of the big picture window and blurt out, "Elsie, I love this room — it's the prettiest and most relaxing I've ever known." It is — large, unpretentious, tastefully done with her harmonious touches. My comment draws a happy laugh and a smile.

We live in a delightful private setting overlooking a captivating wooded area, barely hiding the rocky and pristine Maury River. We retreat to our small, inviting deck for morning coffee. The sun sneaks its warmth to our tidy overlook. White billowy clouds cruise under a vast umbrella of blue sky. A nearby waterfall adds a soothing sound. There we enjoy the frisky antics of squirrels bounding from tree to tree, the stirring sight of a flashy cardinal, the occasional glimpse of a deer or an ambling groundhog. There we talk and plot our day. She reads her daily spiritual guide. We await reddened leaves spattering groundward — a reminder of Vermont.

Afternoons we usually retreat to the Chessie Nature Trail, just steps away, for daily exercise. The broad, winding path follows the meandering Maury with its old canal locks for nine magic miles. On one side towering, craggy cliffs look down on nature's picture of harmony. Shade trees and wildflowers abound equally. An occasional bench provides a scenic stop and a spot for good conversation. We always return home on an upbeat note. Now and then nearby Goshen Pass, Woods Creek Park, and the matchless campus of Washington and Lee University provide similar satisfaction. Life is good.

Epilogue

When England grew corrupt, God brought over a
number of pious persons, and planted them in New
England, and this land was planted with a noble
vine.

JONATHAN EDWARDS

The Finney family traveled from England and arrived in Plymouth Colony in the late 1630s. According to the account of Clifford L. Stott there were "two brothers, John and Robert, two sisters, Katherine and Anne, and their aged mother." Their father may have died at sea. Mr. Stott indicates that a son, John, was born to John Finney on December 24, 1638. In referring to the father, Mr. Stott writes, "Married three times, he produced an extensive posterity." I have the three times in common with my illustrious ancestor, but not the extensive posterity. Presumably I came to my station through divorces and he through passings.

It has been said that there are only two lasting bequests we can give our children and grandchildren. One is roots; the other, wings. As parents we plant the seeds, nourish the roots, and provide sturdy wings on which our children can soar through the future. We hope they will turn to faith and prayers to guide and sustain their flight through life.

There are days when the flight is marked by turbulence.

My middle-class parents and grandparents started something right for me and my two brothers. They planted seeds and sunk roots for us to build on. In our situation it was a single mother who was the real cultivator. When we spread our wings we flew in different directions. My older brother saw the worst of war, became a successful banker and an avid stamp collector, and carries on the conservative wing of the family.

My younger brother's accomplishments are many in the field of urban planning and development, seeking innovative solutions. He is a recipient of the prestigious Philadelphia Award given to the person who has done the most and best to advance the largest interests of the community. He brings more liberal leanings to the family. Both are warm, outgoing, and caring individuals.

Jane Brooks, writes in her book, *Midlife Orphan*, that in middle life we often begin to "reshape our lives to fit new circumstances. Some find new relationships. Some find a resurgence of creative energy and discover new passions and hobbies." How true. I found them all.

I have often felt that my decision to find a new way of life in the late seventies put me onto the path I was meant to walk. There have been too many answers to my prayers to think it coincidence. My mother had an uncanny ability to shore me up at critical times through prayers and with loving support.

I believe the greatest void in my life was the lack of a partner who shared my approach to life. That prayer, like many others, was answered out of the blue. It's a little late, but now I have that life companion, that sharing and caring, that commitment — that true happiness. I have found it in the consummate love of my life. Thank you, Lord. Thank you, Elsie.

Booth Tarkington once said: "Cherish all your happy memories. They make a fine cushion for old age." I have many and will make more. Every day is another start for a loving and abundant life. So to roots and wings, I add a simple prayer. Set me free from the past I cannot change. Grant me your grace and guidance to grow more in your likeness.

Our thoughts often return to our beloved Vermont heritage. We will share our final resting place there in harmony with Him.

At the Close

I like to feel, ere life is through
Although I've failed at times to do
What moralists consider right,
I haven't yet quite lost the fight
Though groping blindly in the dark
There still is left a tiny spark
To help along and light the way,
Renewing faith from day to day.

I like to think it's not for naught
This battle with myself I've fought,
To conquer lust and blot out sin,
No matter what the past has been
If I can only be sincere,
And sleep with mind and conscience clear,
Hope on and strive where things appall,
It's worth the effort after all.

I like to try and forge ahead
Put snap in work ere life has fled;
Yet if I fail to gain the goal,
God grant me strength and self control;
Build up my character and so
In grace and goodness I may grow
Unfolding petals like a rose,
Then I'll be happy at the close.

FRANK LENT

Acknowledgments

Lee quote: *Reminiscences, Anecdotes, and Letters of General Robert E. Lee* by J. William Jones, D. Appleton & Company, New York, 1874. Page 163.

Vermont Design for Education, 1970. Dr. Harvey Scribner, Education Commissioner.

Tidings, 1996, Harrisonburg Mennonite Church, Harrisonburg, Virginia. Joe Mast, Editor.

The Finney Family of Lenton, Nottinghamshire, and Plymouth, Massachusetts by Clifford L. Stott, Genealogist, Orem, Utah, 1994.

"At the Close" by Frank Lent. *Frank Lent's Book of Original Poetry, 1928.* Gift to my mother.

Photographs

Colonnade — Washington and Lee University
Cocker Spaniels — Andre Studio, Lexington, Virginia
Dwight D. Eisenhower — United Press International

With Thanks

to
My wife, my family, my extended families,
and friends, and to all who have made
life richer for knowing them;
and
with my special thanks to
Peter and David for their encouragement,
and to Kristin, Robin, and Jane for
making *Fine Tuning* possible.